AFTER*zen*

Also by Janwillem van de Wetering

Thomas Dunne Books
St. Martin's Griffin   🐾   *New York*

AFTER*zen*

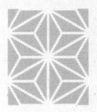

*Experiences
of a Zen
Student Out
on His Ear*

JANWILLEM VAN DE WETERING

THOMAS DUNNE BOOKS.
An imprint of St. Martin's Press.

AFTERZEN: EXPERIENCES OF A ZEN STUDENT OUT ON HIS EAR. Copyright © 1999
by Janwillem van de Wetering. All rights reserved. Printed in the United States of
America. No part of this book may be used or reproduced in any manner what-
soever without written permission except in the case of brief quotations embod-
ied in critical articles or reviews. For information, address St. Martin's Press, 175
Fifth Avenue, New York, N.Y. 10010.

www.stmartins.com

Book design by Ellen R. Sasahara

Library of Congress Cataloging-in-Publication Data

Van de Wetering, Janwillem.
    Afterzen: experiences of a Zen student out on his ear. /
Janwillem van de Wetering.
        p.   cm.
    ISBN 0-312-20493-0 (hc)
    ISBN 0-312-27261-8 (pbk)
    1. Religious life—Zen Buddhism.   I. Title.   II. Title: After Zen
BQ9286 .V36 1999
294.3'927'092—dc21
[B]   99-20107
                                                            CIP

First St. Martin's Griffin Edition: March 2001

10 9 8 7 6 5 4 3 2 1

To Danny C. Gordon and Walter Nowick

AUTHOR'S NOTE

All the koans in *Afterzen* are from reputable sources, most of them appearing in two or more of the following collections in various but similar phrasing:

Blyth, R. H. *Zen and Zen Classics, vol. 4: Mumonkan.* The Hokuseido Press: Tokyo, 1966.

Hofman, Yoel. *The Sound of One Hand Clapping: 281 Zen Koans with Answers.* Basic Books: New York, 1974.

Nowick, Walter. *The Wisteria Tangle.* Sunstone Press: Santa Fe, 1971.

Sekida, Katsuki. *Two Zen Classics: Mumonkan and Hekiganroku.* Weatherhill: New York and Tokyo, 1977.

CONTENTS

AFTER*zen*

THE GOOD-BYE KOAN

Koans are vastly overrated. A Hindu teacher, whom I will call Baba, an Indian (from India) in whites whom I met at the Boston airport during a long snowbound wait, told me that. But then he might have been overrated himself. There's a lot of competition in religion. Jealousy too. Jealousy is a fact of life. One of my Zen teachers told me that, shortly before his center collapsed and we, the disciples, were out in the big bad world again. Most of us left the area, never to be heard of again, but, riding in a small plane over the Maine woods, I found one of my former buddies.

This man, whom I will call Ben-san, had once been an idealist, and in the idealist sixties had traveled to Japan to study Zen. By happenstance he went to the same temple I did, but we missed each other; I left a few weeks before he arrived. Meeting him later in America was quite an event, for we knew all the same people back in Kyoto. Same abbot, same head monk, same regular monks. Same bars in Kyoto's famous Willow Quarter, which we visited on our off nights.

Like me, Ben stayed a few years in the Japanese Zen temple, was given the Mu koan, never passed it, and left. There were other similarities: same age; we were both white males from Protestant, in his case fundamentalist, backgrounds; we were both drinking men. There seemed to be a similar artistry in both of us that pushed him into creating pagodas in oriental-style gardens and me to write tales and build junk sculptures when my back needed stretching.

In America, in the early seventies, we both finished up with the same teacher, whom I'll only call Sensei here. Sensei had spent many years in Japan and, according to the Zen grapevine, "had his insights confirmed by qualified authorities." Ben and I enrolled at Sensei's North American center as students of Zen koans and practitioners of the wayless way.

Those were the same koans that "Baba," the Indian guru at Logan Airport, said he had studied from a Hindu point of view and found, with some exceptions, somewhat clever, a trifle contrived, and definitely wanting. He smiled forgivingly. "Given the reputation of Zen, I had really expected a little more." I had to laugh. Those were the exact words Sensei liked to use after a strenuous week of meditation, but he would stay it sternly. Sensei always seemed genuinely disappointed at the failures of his students.

Among the travelers hanging out at Logan Airport during a blizzard, with all chairs taken and the bathrooms overflowing, Baba stood out as an exceptional-looking man. Always eager to learn, I approached this figure in flowing robes below and flowing hair on top.

"Are you a guru, sir?"

"For sure." Baba spoke with a clipped, high-pitched Indian accent. "Are you a truth seeker?"

"I used to be a Zen student, sir."

"You gave up?"

"Not on my questions, sir."

"But on Zen you gave up?"

"Not really, sir. But I seem to be on my own now."

Baba nodded. He knew all about Zen. The practice of *zazen*, meditation, and koan study, solving of dharma riddles while facing a teacher at *sanzen*, the early morning meeting in the master's temple.

I said that was what I had been doing for many years, evenings and weekends, for I usually worked in day jobs. "How come you are a guru, Baba?"

He looked at me loftily, from under impressively tufted eyebrows. Had I misaddressed this evolved being? I didn't mean offense. "Shrih Baba? Shrih Baba Maharaj? You have a title, sir? Your Holiness, maybe?"

He smiled and bowed. "Never mind my titles. Holy titles are all hogwash, my friend."

I liked that. It was the sort of thing Bodhidharma would have said to the emperor of China, before stalking out of the imperial palace to meditate for another nine years in his cave.

A fresh foot of snow was covering Boston's runways. Baba had time to chat. He told me he felt comfortable in airports, for he had started his own career at an airport too, at JFK in New York. As a pre-guru, Baba was an illegal alien and cleaned restaurant tables for a living. This was, again, the sixties, a spiritual time. America developed a demand for esoteric teachers. The law of demand and supply made holy men enter the country. Busboy Baba noticed that the teachers flocking into JFK from his native country wore white clothes and had much facial hair. They were

Hindus. They had big expressive eyes and sharp features. They quoted the *Bhagavad Gita*. They recited mantras, Sanskrit syllables charged with holy power, and held their hands in certain ways, a practice known as doing *mudras*. They were invariably met by well-dressed ladies and their long-haired male attendants, couples who had expensive cars waiting for them in the airport parking lot.

"What," Baba asked me, "prevented me from declaring myself a guru?" The title is not protected. Baba had shareable insights galore, gathered in previous lives and from the poverty and pain of the present. In order to show his true status he needed a white dhoti and matching jacket, and sandals to show off his muscular long toes—items that weren't hard to get. The other requirements were already rightfully his. He had been raised in a priestly, Brahmin, top-class (albeit starving) family, knew Hindu scripture by heart, kept up a home altar, burned incense and performed daily prostrations. He even meditated from time to time, although meditation, Baba told me, is not all it's cracked up to be. When overdone it gives you a pain in the ass. Had I noticed?

I had. Prolonged zazen gave me chronic hemorrhoids. Baba told me the human body is not designed to sit in the double or even the half lotus position for long periods of time. The postures put excessive strain on the rectum. I found that easy to believe. Preparation H is a staple in Zen monasteries, together with Maalox, for eating too hot meals too fast, peer pressure by zealots, too little sleep, and the relentless master's constant urging to solve a koan create mental tensions that ulcerate Zen stomachs.

"Right," Baba said. "Forget all that. Your own precious Buddha told his disciples to walk the middle way, to avoid excess."

"No spiritual practice?"

"Just daily life," Baba said. "Apply some awareness. Take daily time to perform a short ritual of your choice, but mostly just

be, my friend." He dropped his voice and stared at me hypnoti-
cally. "Just be."

"But what about suffering?"

He shrugged. "What about it?"

I told him suffering wasn't nice.

"Do you suffer?" Baba asked me.

I told him I was doing just fine, thank you. Being fairly well
off seemed to be my karma. I shouldn't be complaining—heaven
forbid—but my habitual fate could be, at times, a bit boring.
Whatever I did, wherever I went, I always seemed to be doing
just fine. Look at me now: new tweed jacket and just the right
zippered mud boots, a four-wheel-drive vehicle in good repair
parked at my home airport, a wonderful wife waiting in a comfortable house on landscaped acres, okay income, overall good
health, the complete recordings of Miles Davis, and good sound
equipment shelved next to the word processor. Now look at other
people. I showed Baba a two-page color photo of the coast of
Bangladesh, printed in a magazine I had just bought. Recent
floods had caused numberless people and cattle to drown; when
the sea receded the coast was set off by a white line consisting of
dead people in their white cotton clothes, and a brown line consisting of dead cattle, going on for miles.

"So?" Baba asked.

"The suffering of these Bangladeshians makes me doubt."

"Doubt what?"

"Whether there is a purpose."

"To suffering?"

"Yes," I said, "to life."

"A purpose to life?" Baba patted my shoulder. "There isn't
any."

"So all this is just painful chaos?"

Baba raised a hand to draw my attention, then recited in his high voice, "There is no suffering, no cause of suffering, no cessation of suffering . . ."

". . . and no path," I said.

"You know the Heart Sutra," Baba said. "It's not Hindu, but Buddhism is Indian too and all Buddha did was revive part of our original religion. And you're right. No path, forget 'path.' 'Path' is highly overrated."

I was beginning to like Baba. He seemed to be a master of the Far Eastern method of negation. *Neti, neti.* That what is not. Destroy all constructions, then enjoy empty space. "You have a temple?" I asked.

He had one, in the Catskills, but advised that there was not much there for me. I should make use of my present lack of status. Why get interested in yet another inflicted discipline? Baba, at his spiritual center, was merely keeping people busy by providing them with a nonharmful routine, such as limited meditation and chanting of scripture. The place was partly run as a farm so there was work to help deal with depression and stress. Rules were structured to keep disciples upright. Everyone was to wear white dhotis and jackets and open-toed sandals while on the grounds (most disciples came for the weekend, sometimes also for "training weeks"). There was to be no frolicking with any abusable substance, no guitar music after hours, no dillydallying except for those with guru or guru-escort status, no excessive donations to buy being-teacher's-pet, and during farewell ceremonies (in private, when disciples left the center to go home for a while) he would hand out praise and cookies.

"Chocolate chip," Baba said. "Don't care for them myself, but Americans associate them with parental loving guidance. British disciples I give digestive biscuits."

"You bake your presents yourself?"

Baba bought them at Stop & Shop.

There was some slyness about him that I, coming from a trading background in the Holland city of Rotterdam, thought I recognized. I tried to phrase a respectful inquiry as to whether Baba was into money perhaps. Shearing his silly sheep. He cut me short as soon as I used the word *money*.

"You mean Greed?" An interesting impediment, but he had given it up. There was the temptation, for he had been poor for so long. He did indulge during his early days on his spiritual health farm. Baba drove a Jaguar for a while, ate gourmet, charged high prices for special interviews, obtained tax-free status, even increased his income by operating a health-food restaurant that was staffed with disciple labor at no cost, but an overdose of material success had made him nervous. He closed the restaurant and reduced the contributions that his disciples paid on a monthly basis. The Jaguar was driven by "my number-one lady" now, who used it for community shopping. Baba rode a bicycle, as back in Calcutta, but this one was a ten-speed.

"And sex?"

"Sex." He nodded wisely. "There is that, too."

I told him that sexual desire, first frustrated, later perverted, had helped bring down the Buddhist center where I had studied. Baba kept nodding sympathetically. He could understand that. After all, a holy man is still a man and a man has needs. He didn't want to go to Manhattan for his needs. It was nicer if sex came to him at his temple. He never meant to be a self-denying recluse. One young lady had wrapped herself in gift paper and rolled into his quarters in a shopping cart pushed by two girlfriends in bikinis. Was it wrong if an enlightened teacher accepts the gift of an attractive disciple's ego? Ego is the mask that has to come off to show pure being. Only in pure being can divine insight be clear.

Sensei used to say, "If you present me with your beautiful mind, why can't I have your beautiful body?" I told Baba.

"How interesting," Baba said. "Now tell me about the koans you managed to solve during your many years of Zen practice, my friend."

There was no time; a runway had opened up and Baba's plane was waiting. He gave me his card. "Come and see me sometime." He caressed my shoulder. "But don't bring me your personal problems. I cannot help people carry their ego loads." He squeezed my hand. "I don't want to, either."

Off he went, a bundle of human light. Wouldn't it be fun to spend time at his chocolate-chip-cookie heaven? But no. Baba was probably right. It's hard for a man in his fifties to dance in the meadow again, pleasing Daddy and his numbered egoless escorts.

Didn't I feel contented on my own now? Doing exactly what Baba recommended: using daily life as my practice, my *sadana*, chanting the Heart Sutra at my altar every morning, burning incense to the little plastic skeleton of a dinosaur, an extinct being, like *Homo sapiens* would be pretty soon, that I kept in an open box between ritual candles?

I hadn't minded leaving the Buddhist center, but I sometimes missed my pals, especially Ben-san. I wondered how he was coping.

Suffering is caused by desire, and I definitely wished to see Ben-san again. I wasn't going to make a special effort, but desires, once clearly stated, have a way of being fulfilled, most often within the lifetime.

A technical man in the village had built himself an airplane and asked me, one sunny winter day, to join him for a spin. We flew around Mount Katahdin and, coming back from skimming lakes and rivers and crossing vast areas of wild woods, spotted a pagoda not too far from the Purple Hill airstrip. My pilot friend circled the structure and found a long, winding track that led to it. We were both impressed. The pagoda was a mini version of what I recognized as a famous Kyoto temple. It had three stories with what appeared to be living quarters on the first. There was also a landscaped garden, in outline visible under the snow. I could detect what would be moss patches around decorative giant boulders that would no doubt show glowing orange and yellow lichens once the thaw set in. There was also a flat, some forty-foot-square, slightly rippled area with three rocks off-center that looked as though it would be raked daily during the milder part of the year. There was a frozen pond where I guessed large multicolored carp would be hibernating under the ice. A very Zenlike landscape. The pilot had known Ben-san, too. "Must be Ben's. So that's where he hides out now." We circled the pagoda again, much lower than the legal five hundred feet, and we saw a man come out, waving a shotgun.

"Ben all right," the pilot said.

"Got to walk out there sometime," I said.

The pilot checked his instrument panel and handed me a note with the location's coordinates. "Shouldn't be hard to find. You can borrow my handheld positioner. The path to there is basically north-south and leads out of Sorry. Starts at Blackberry Brook. Can't miss it if you take a compass and my GPS. Better make sure you don't get shot, though."

Sorry is a suburb of the Maine coastal city of Rotworth, where I have been living for a good while now. I waited for another good clear day, with the right kind of snow to support my snowshoes. According to my map, the distance out of Sorry would be some ten miles. I left early and got to Ben's pagoda by noon.

He came out with his gun but put it down and hugged me lightly. "You smell better now," he said, "in the zendo you stank."

He ought to know; we used to sit next to each other during bathless weeks. I recalled his fragrance too.

"You're a hermit now?" I asked.

Ben-san said he liked that better than the practice at our Buddhist center. Living alone in the pagoda had also helped him quit drinking. I had quit drinking too. I told him, "Alcohol no longer fulfills my needs." He thought that was a silly way of putting things and probably untrue. "Your wife confronted you. Told you either you quit or she left. Now you need a macho excuse. Always trying to impress the audience. Haven't changed much, have you?"

"So what do you do for money now, Ben?"

Very little, he told me. He wasn't always at the pagoda. He worked some of his summers, away in New Hampshire, staying with employers for free, saving some dollars. Spring, fall, and winter he stacked up on staples and hermited away, surrounded by wildlife.

There were several jays around, a squirrel or two, a tribe of chickadees, some juncos. I saw that there were feeders placed in strategic spots, designed like little temples. Ben-san was still bitten by the building bug. He looked lonely to me.

"Get a woman," I said. "Some pleasant and caring soul tired of being abused by her sadistic boyfriend. Pick her up late, some Friday night at the Lazy Loon in Rotworth. You'll be king of the castle. Those women haven't seen a sober man in years."

He didn't care for making women happy.

"Male soul mate, perhaps? A charming disciple?"

He told me he had given up on people. Ben-san the misanthrope. He crossed his arms defensively. I left him to his posturing and admired his backdrop. The pagoda was an impressive structure, built from hand-hewn mismatched logs, dovetailed together like a Chinese puzzle. All wooden pegs, no nails anywhere. The intricate handiwork must have consumed months of lonely winter time. The delicately sloping roofs were covered with old-fashioned cedar shakes, cut with a giant chisel. A jewel in the woods. I bowed and recited the ancient Tibetan mantra. *Om mani padme hum,* Hail to the jewel in the lotus.

"Never understood what that meant," Ben told me.

"Still doing Zen practice?" I asked when he finally uncrossed his arms.

He nodded. "Sure."

"Zazen?"

Some zazen. Not too much. "I never liked it. Half an hour in the morning, half an hour in the evening. That's all I can put up with now. That endless Zen sitting never did shit for me."

I noticed a Direct TV dish on the pagoda's top roof and a rusted Honda generator in a lean-to.

"I follow the cult-movie channel." Ben-san said. "Some opera, too. Not for too long on end. It's hard to carry in the gas for the generator."

I didn't believe him. There were several fifty-five-gallon drums away from the building, under their own roof, and I spotted a sled and an old but functional-looking snowmobile. Ben-san is a powerfully built man—it wouldn't trouble him even to hand-pull a heavy load for ten miles.

I hadn't given up on peer pressure yet. "Still do koan study? Must be hard without Sensei telling you what's what."

"Sensei." He shrugged. "Good riddance of twisted nonsense."

"But you still work on a koan, Ben?"

The arms were crossed again against a puffed-up chest. "What's my koan study to you?"

"But Ben-san, we are dharma brothers." I reminded him how far back we went. How we had been drinking buddies. How we had sworn to use each other's lives as mirrors. "Sake for two," I sang to the tea-for-two tune while I skipped around him.

He unfroze a bit. Just one koan he was still working on, Ben told me over baked beans and tofu over rice with chili sauce and pickled daikon. The one he had received some months before Sensei's hermitage went back to nature. Students aren't supposed to discuss their koans but as Ben and I had both been released, we could consider ourselves free now. "Tell me about your last koan," I said, thinking I might show some superiority here. Not that he would want to be helped out. Zen students consider themselves the cream of the Buddhist crop, those who walk the steep short way. We are potential high-class bodhisattvas—just one more koan and we can step into nirvana.

"Tell me your koan, dear Ben-san."

"Nah."

Okay. I was on the pagoda's front steps, nudging my boots into my snowshoes. The hell with Mr. Do-It-Himself. He could rot in his pagoda. It was a nice building, though. I had told Ben his creation reminded me of a toy pagoda my mother brought back from Indonesia, in the twenties, from the "Dutch Indies," as she still called the country.

The little pagoda had been crafted out of an elephant tooth and had, like Ben-san's, three stories. My mother said she had bought it at the Borobudur, Java's great Buddhist temple covering an entire hilltop, an elaborate piece of architecture abandoned after Buddhism was replaced by Islam. Each story had a set of tiny hinged doors. I liked to open them and peer inside. There had been Buddha statues in each compartment but as they could be taken out, they got lost. My mother bewailed their disappearance but a Chinese Buddhist friend told us the pagoda made more sense without its former tenants. "Form is emptiness. Better to show nothing."

Ben-san's pagoda's second and third stories were empty too.

They didn't even have doors. The wind passed freely under their swept-up roofs. Only the lower floor was walled in, insulated, and fitted with doors and storm doors. "I've got to live somewhere," Ben told me, showing me his sparse furniture. He was frowning again. "You still fill up all your outbuildings with possessions? The villa? The double garage? The studios? The gazebo? The guest house?"

He knew what he was talking about. He had designed and built my compound. In those days he needed more money, to finance travels during the Zen training's off seasons, and I kept providing him with work.

"Thanks for the tofu," I said. "Bye now."

He held me back. "I'm working on the bull koan."

There are probably a dozen bull koans in use in the various Zen sects. "Which bull?"

"Why can't-the-tail-pass-by bull koan," Ben-san said. "It's driving me crazy."

Koans are designed to drive the Zen student crazy. I kicked off my snowshoes and allowed Ben to guide me back into his living quarters. We had coffee.

"Gozo En Zenji," I said. "That's the Zen master Sensei was quoting. I remember Gozo's tale. Something to do with you're in the sanzen room, early in the morning, and Sensei is confronting you, squatting on his cushions wearing the Japanese roshi gown he had outgrown since he gained weight. He points at the small window above his head. He tells you that it's like 'Gozo's water-buffalo bull, passing by that window—his huge head, his big horns, his four feet go by, but that's it, the tail never shows up. What of that, eh?'"

"Right," Ben said. "So you were on that koan too?"

Ben-san and I, during our student days, were probably always on the same koans.

Now, what are koans? They are riddles that are deliberately

phrased obscurely. There are pieces missing. No Zen student, not two thousand years ago in China, not a thousand years ago in Japan, not today in the Maine woods or in a California valley or on an Arizona mesa, can make sense of any given koan until the teacher does some explaining first. And he won't. He wants you to squirm in stupidity. Sensei himself, when I knew him in Japan where he was an advanced disciple with much seniority and many years of sanzen behind him, complained about koans, calling them "word mazes." He was working on a long story that involved a white crane, and a white crane means something in Chinese mythology (I forget now what it means) and if you don't know what it means you'll never figure out what the white crane is doing in that long koan, and you won't solve the Zen riddle. In Sensei's case, his Japanese teacher didn't know that Sensei, an American, didn't know about the esoteric meaning of "white crane," so master and student were butting their heads together in the sanzen room and "precious time was lost." At the time I thought that that complaint made no sense either. Was Sensei in a hurry? Did he want his degree tomorrow? Was he eager to hang out his shingle as a teacher himself?

Sensei probably did. Ben-san, however, never showed any interest in a Buddhist career. Most likely he just wanted to know things, like if there was a purpose to him being born into a fundamentalist Protestant community that served a harsh and unforgiving divinity Ben only wanted to get away from. And what was the miracle of life, which he, with his love of wildlife and beautiful structures, felt he was close to, but could never grab hold of, not even after the third jug of sake? Why the Vietnam War? Why the need to pollute a perfectly good planet? Every time he was given a new koan he thought the answer might solve his quest, but there was always another mountain on the horizon. The bull koan was the last one he ever meant to work on. He absolutely had to know the answer. Did I have it?

"Your bull koan is an overrated koan," I told Ben-san. "It's not like the Mu koan, or *The Sound of One Hand*. The tail-of-the-bull-koan has nothing to do with Nothing. It does not indicate the great void. It doesn't comprise the entire Heart Sutra into a single negation. It's your final koan and it's minor."

"So how do *you* know?" Ben asked. "Did you pass the damned thing?"

"But there is nothing to pass," I said. "It's just a little illustration of a problem that won't go away. You know what 'tail' stands for in Chinese mythology?"

"Something to wag?"

I shook my head. If this had been sanzen and if I had been the Zen master throning on cushions stacked on a platform and Ben had been the disciple groveling below on the tatami, I would have picked up my little bell and shaken it and he would have to prostrate himself three times and leave and be back the next day, bright and early.

"Close," I said. "It's something to get stuck with. The idea 'tail,' in Far Eastern symbolism, means 'ego,' 'personality.' The tail stands for 'being-me-ness,' and no incarnated spirit, whether he comes as the Dalai Lama, or as Allen Ginsberg, Christ, you, the latest U.S. president, or me, can get away from the personality we happen to come equipped with. Cradle to grave, it's always there, constantly changing but never quite fading out. Concern for Number One can't help holding us back. I'm not going to cut my tail off, at best I can try being aware that I'm tied down by the appendage."

"Did you read that somewhere?"

Sure I read that somewhere. Zen doesn't believe in books, but there were forty thousand Zen books in print in Asia before the West started multiplying that figure. Most "official" Zen books, that is, most treatises published by qualified masters, list and somehow explain koans, a few quite openly. There's *The*

Sound of One Hand, two hundred eighty-one koans and their answers, a work compiled by a genuine Zen master in 1916, and commented on by several genuine Zen masters since (some say it can do no harm; others say it should be burned), translated by the scholar Yoel Hoffmann, published by Basic Books in New York, in 1975. The original version of this telltale book was bought up and destroyed by several Tokyo Zen masters, but the publisher printed new editions. There was, and is, *The Green Grotto Record,* with a hundred koans explained by Zen masters Engo and Dai-e, tenth and eleventh centuries, and available in at least two English translations. There are *Mumonkan* and *Kekiganroku,* two classic koan collections translated and demystified by Katsuki Sekida, and published by Weatherhill in 1977. Big buffalo bulls and their restraining tails perform in these works.

"It was Sensei's parting koan," I told Ben. "He was saying good-bye to us, his first disciples, whom he knew in Japan and who followed him out here to the Sorry hermitage. It shows that Zen teachers have egos, and that he was no exception. Sensei wanted us to know that all he did so blatantly wrong could not be helped. He excused his flopped show here. He showed us, by the bull's tail that would never pass the light of the enlightenment window, that part of him was stuck in the mud."

"So what is the correct answer?" Ben asked, for all "little" koans have single correct answers. You've got to give them before the teacher of the Rinzai Sect, the sect that Sensei belonged to, releases you from the present stage of insight and provides the next "little" koan, which may clear up another minor aspect of Mu, the gateless gate, the subject of the real, the basic, riddle. ("Does the puppy dog have Buddha nature too?" the monk inquired of the priest Joshu. The priest said, "Mu," meaning "No.")

The correct passing answer?

"What you do," I told Ben, "is you shuffle a little closer to the platform, on your knees, smiling politely, and then you reach out, behind Sensei, and you give a terrific jerk on his robe, so that he almost tumbles over backward, and you say "Well now, you're pretty well stuck yourself, aren't you, old boy?"

"That's all?"

That was all.

It was time to leave the pagoda. Ben put on his snowshoes too, and accompanied me a little way on the path to the village of Sorry. "So it was Sensei's good-bye koan, was it? His ego had pretty much tripped him up, broken his career as a teacher, and he wasn't going to waste any more of our time and effort? Or of his?"

"Possibly," I said.

"You don't know for sure?"

I said I had made it up. I knew nothing for sure. And I wished Ben-san "Bless Buddha." He turned back. It had started snowing heavily again.

What Happened to Harry?

Some people are particularly gifted at Zen study. They learn Japanese and/or Chinese in a year, never move in meditation, and, in the case of uniformed monks, look good in robes that they patch themselves. They are naturals. They know things before you tell them.

Jonathan, I think the natural's name was, Jonathan Smith-hyphen-something, was a tall, handsome man with a full blond beard and piercing blue eyes. He was also British, born in a castle, and raised at proper schools, which gave him the right to use an upper-class accent. He told me he had developed an interest in philosophy when he came in contact with the lower classes and was particularly interested in Buddhism, as Buddha had been a prince too. Jonathan's father had gambled away the family fortune, but Jonathan managed to support himself in style. He showed up while we were digging holes on the Maine Zen farm, deep holes for fruit trees guaranteed to last through thirty below zero. Sensei had plans to sell plums to the local market in years to come. There was little enthusiasm on the part of his immediate students, as they had learned that none of the master's experimental schemes ever worked out. When he noticed their unwillingness in the orchard project, he called on his "outside" students, those who did not live on the farm and who worked in the real world to make money to support their families, to donate weekends and spare time. Jonathan, a guest student, was suddenly digging next to me, using a long-handled spade as if he had done it for years.

"This is useless work," I told Jonathan, "for the trees will die, all of them, come January." January always has a few nights when the temperature dips to fifty below zero. Jonathan grinned. "Dust to dust, right, old chap? Soon a meteor will hit the old planet, but we still keep busy, don't we, sport?" He kept digging. The new arrival to our Zen group was wearing a white cotton coverall and the sort of hat that I had seen on the head of the jazz player Lester Young: flat, stylish, elegant, odd. The coverall was stylish too. "Where do you get those clothes?" It turned out that Jonathan was a used-clothes dealer. He bought in bulk from the U.S. Salvation Army, then had his containers shipped to London, where he sorted, washed, repaired, dry-cleaned, and sold to thrift shops all over the United Kingdom. Special items he sold on Tottingham Court Road Market, in London. Of course, he said, he didn't do any actual work himself. He had the work done; there was no money in work, but there was money in trading and to keep his hand in, he sometimes manned the London outlet himself, bellowing at an amazed public in his Shakespearean tones. "Making an oddity of myself helps to lure the buyers, you know, old chap. Sometimes I play the trumpet and my regular Tottingham man is from Jamaica, unbeatable on percussion. We perform ballads to bring them in, marches to make them reach for the wallet."

Jonathan planned to stay a month at the Maine hermitage to see what koan solving might be all about. He stayed in a nearby air-conditioned motel and rented a brand-new Jeep to commute. The community's women were much taken by his elegant presence, which made most of the males wary of him. He did flatter us all, though, and ruffled feathers gradually got brushed down. In addition to excelling at the social graces needed to survive in cramped quarters, Jonathan had no trouble with the actual practice. For old Zen hands it's always a joy to see newcomers suffer, their aching bodies twisted painfully on hard cushions, but Jonathan did effortless zazen, apparently on an invisible cloud cushion of his own making. He didn't even bother to stretch his legs during breaks. Sensei seemed eager to get him to join us permanently and invited him over for dinner and private concerts. Sensei on cello, Jonathan on trumpet, they played variations on themes by Satie. Jonathan, who often worked with me, told me to be wary of Sensei. Our teacher reminded him of an abbot he had met during another spiritual outing, in Nevada, where black-robed and heavily bewhiskered religious monks in exile had set up a thriving monastery that lived well on raising large numbers of fat turkeys. One of Jonathan's grandmothers was Russian and he had always felt attracted to the Russian cross, Rasputin beards, "the dark passion of longing to be saved from ignorance," as he put it, until the outcome of his Nevada experience had turned his mind to the limitless void of anarchy that he planned to experience at the end of the Buddhist path.

"I no longer want the illusion to make sense," he told me while digging holes for Sensei's ill-fated plum trees. "I want to accept life as senseless now." He put in the stammer that educated

Englishmen like to use when setting up a new theory. "But I still have some trouble with that. So I thought I'd look at what you Zen chaps came up with. You know? That it is all illusion? Not to hold on to any explanation? Fuck values? Be free?"

I was still contemplating his Russian grandmother's darkly religious goal. To be gloomily saved from ignorance?

"But isn't there supposed to be *light* in our longing for freedom?" I asked. "Doesn't *ignorance* stand for darkness? Those Russian monks of yours have it the wrong way round."

"Russia thrives on being wrong," Jonathan said. "Why wouldn't a different path not be valid? The laughing Buddha, the crying Christian saint. What does it matter how you get there? Don't all religions aim for the top of the mountain? My grandmother didn't really want to see the light; she wanted to wallow in dark shadows. She liked to wail. She played orthodox psalms on the balalaika and got choked up in tears while she tried to sing along. As a child, whenever she looked bored, I would shout 'Fyodor Dostoyevsky' to make her melt, once again, in the glory of being homesick. Or someone would wag a finger at her and say '*Nyet*'—no. Not having things made Grandmother happy. She would only say '*Da*'—yes—to confirm she was in pain." He rested on his spade's handle. "Besides, your teacher seems rather a gloomy sort too."

"You don't like Sensei?"

Jonathan shrugged. Like, dislike, he wasn't going to be tempted to express any values. "He reminds me of Father Stanislas, not a nice man, you know, definitely not your uncle. He affected handing out pleasantries, he could put on a kindly face, like Sensei when he pours Kentucky sipping whisky after playing the cello. But he wanted to see your pain, your sorrow."

I insisted. "Sensei doesn't seem loving to you? Like he wants to share his insights? He isn't a blessed spirit, qualified to enter the unlimited blessings of the void, but he doesn't because he wants to save all the sentient beings first? He makes the ultimate sacrifice?"

Jonathan was familiar with the bodhisattva ideal. Saving all others first is a Zen vow. There is no way to get Zen insight if the student plans on enlightening himself only. The trick is to forego that kind of reward. Only the selfless pass through the eye of the needle. "No," Jonathan told me again. "Sensei doesn't strike me as a sharer." Like Father Stanislas, Sensei, Jonathan thought, had been tricked by some demon to exploit his position of temporary power. "Disciples make good slaves."

Jonathan told me about his stay with the monks in Nevada after another business journey, when he had bought tons of clothing from the Los Angeles Salvation Army. In order to cleanse his greedy soul (and lustful, too—he had hired a showgirl in Las Vegas for private shows), he had gone to the mountain monastery, partly, possibly, in memory of Gramma's dark longings. He had liked his spiritual adventure in the Nevada hills at first. There was the surrounding desert, and he had walked between giant cactus plants and been sniffed at by a curious coyote. He had prayed in his cell with the moon behind his barred window. He liked the food: home-baked loaves of dark bread, fried cactus and turkey eggs with elaborate salads. The monkish bean soup was a delicacy. He thought he might have felt "the dark passion" that goes with "to be saved from ignorance." "But then the sheriff talked to me in town." Jonathan went to town every few days to smoke cigars and look at cowgirls driving battered pickup trucks. "I'm not really after having religious experiences, old chap. Wouldn't know how to handle a holy vision." Jonathan was sitting on a hotel's balcony and the sheriff showed up, sat next to him, how-de-doo'd the stranger like in good B movies, chewed tobacco, spat without hitting his snakeskin boots. The sheriff was a big man with tinted sideburns wearing a Stetson, khakis, a huge sidearm in a holster. "He said he heard I was staying at the commie monastery and could I please help find out what happened to Harry."

I stopped digging holes for the plum trees that would freeze to death that winter, all hundred and fifty of them, bought out of the contributions of Sensei's disciples.

Jonathan and I drank tea from Jonathan's Thermos behind a juniper bush as his tale unfolded. Harry was a friendly monk who would go shopping once a week to buy his monastery's staples. Harry spoke some English. The kids loved Harry because he looked like a young Father Christmas and could juggle a stack of telephone books, pretending to be clumsy, dropping the heavy volumes but catching them with his foot and kicking them backward, where he would grab them casually as he pretended to scratch his butt. Harry was laughs, but he stopped coming to town and his replacement got nervous when questioned about Harry. Harry who?

What happened to Harry the telephone book juggler, the sheriff asked. Would Jonathan make some inquiries? Weren't the British and Americans allies? Hadn't they been going to war together lately? The sheriff would sure appreciate some allied help.

"This was before the Berlin Wall came down," Jonathan told me. "Eastern Europeans were still considered to be pathologically unstable. Father Stanislas was *very* pathologically unstable."

I saw where this was going. During my studies with the Auxiliary Amsterdam Municipal Police I had run across an essay, in a criminal handbook, titled _On Psychotic Behavior in Isolated Cult Groups_. Cult leaders, the author-psychologist claimed, like to enforce their homemade rules. When these self-appointed dictators exercise power in small isolated groups, there is real danger of criminal behavior. Normally there is some control in larger organizations. Bishops check on abbots. Complaints can be lodged by the lower ranks, religious peons, monks, or nuns, and will be investigated by some kind of religious police. There is church law laying down at least a minimum of mutual understanding and respect for personal freedom. So much for the ideal situation, but in the case of a community away from the mother church, a leader's power tends to become absolute. Regular law enforcement is often not inclined to check on "holy" people who keep to themselves in rural areas. Being beyond the reach of his superiors will make a cult leader swell up into a formidable figure. Absolute power is known to aggravate sadism, which is always present in the human psyche. In unchecked cult groups punishment is often effected by "shunning," where the disobedient victim becomes ignored by the group, or offenders can no longer take part in joint prayers or meditations but have to "work for their salvation on their own," in uncomfortable conditions. Another way to humiliate the obstreperous is to force them to ask forgiveness by kneeling outside the master's quarters for hours before daybreak. It can always get worse. Beatings, torture, starving, and untreated illness have been documented, and in Harry's case it was murder. Harry had displeased Father Stanislas and got kicked by his peers on their superior's orders. "Cracked his ribs and skull. Then the blighters left him to die." Jonathan stared at me. "Not a pretty picture."

"You saw the corpse?"

"Yes. There was an autopsy. Monks confessed. Only Father Satanislas was prosecuted."

"What had Harry done?"

"Made fun of Father Stanislas in public."

"You found the body?" I asked.

No, Jonathan had not, but he had figured out where Harry's remains were hidden because the coyote, which had sniffed him before, kept howling around rocks that were stacked on the unfortunate's shallow grave. "There's always a shallow grave in an amateurish murder," he said gloomily, "and there's always the unrevenged soul clamoring for attention."

Alerted by the insisting coyote, Jonathan had pointed the sheriff in the right direction.

"Don't look nervous, old chap," Jonathan told me. "It all goes with the game. Shouldn't you go for detachment in Zen?" He had read that in Tokyo a young monk had fallen asleep in the meditation hall of a famous Zen temple, fallen forward, and broken his head on the stone floor. Another monk was beaten on the head by a Zen master's short heavy stick. He didn't live either. The masters were never even questioned by the police.

I asked what happened at the trial of Harry's death. Father Stanislas was taken to an asylum for the criminally insane. "He set up a turkey farm there, too, but then he switched to ostriches. Ostriches have more meat and the feathers are extra."

Paranoia swept down. Fattening big birds, I thought. And here we were, offering ourselves for slaughter by fully empowered—by us—Father Sensei.

As Jonathan showed no signs of wanting to be a permanent pupil, Sensei had not started him on a koan. Jonathan kept asking me about koan study. As he was a natural, what with his long and easy meditations and the calmness I could feel in his spirit, an ability to be unruffled by adverse circumstances, the stiff upper lip, his insistence on timely tea (lots of milk and sugar) ceremonies (punctually served twice a day, to whomever he happened to be with), I thought I might try him out on the "spiritual problem" I was struggling with.

Tokusan's Bowl is a long koan. Memorizing long koan stories is a nuisance that comes with Zen study. Sticklers for perfection, and Sensei was one of them, want their disciples to recite the entire koan verbatim, every time there is a meeting between master and a pupil. I had been carrying the story around all winter, waiting outside the sanzen house with mice warming themselves on my bare feet.

This is the problem the bowl koan illustrates, and the student is asked to comment on, so that he may gain insight:

> There is a Zen monastery. Tokusan is the abbot, Seppo is the head monk [abbots teach, head monks are temple managers], and one day the noon meal is late. Tokusan, holding his bowl, enters the hall. Seppo says, "I didn't hear the bell announcing lunch and the gong hasn't been sounded either. Old man with your bowl, what are you doing?"
>
> Tokusan is quiet. He lowers his head and returns to his room. Seppo now tells another monk, Ganto, "Tokusan may be great but he never understood the final verse."

Jonathan came to dinner at my house and I took him to the study afterward. I showed him the koan that I had copied from a Chinese textbook and tacked to the wall. I only recognize a few Chinese hieroglyphs, but having the original characters up there gave me the idea that I was closer to their meaning. I explained that to my guest as I translated the text. "Closer to their meaning."

"You mean closer to their nonmeaning," Jonathan said. "That has to be the clue. Nonmeaning. No value. If you try to get into meaning when you analyze discussions between exemplary Zen men, you're lost straightway."

That was the answer, of course. Part of the answer anyway. I had been tricked, for long cold months and during quite a few uncomfortable meetings with Sensei, to believe that Tokusan was attaching a meaning to his head monk's rude behavior. Tokusan didn't care about meaning; he couldn't or he wouldn't be a free man, qualified to show the way to the unenlightened. How silly of me.

"You thought the old fellow was upset?" Jonathan asked. "Why? Because he 'lowered his head'? You thought he was going to butt this loutish head monk in the chest with his bare skull to show him what is what? I don't think so, not from the context of the scene. Tokusan probably just bowed to acknowledge having received the information that lunch was to be late. And he wasn't going to hang around some drafty dharma hall if he had a cozy room with a soft mattress upstairs. He calmly went back to extend his nap, don't you think?"

Of course. Tokusan was no Father Stanislas who would have Harry kicked to death because he was not being respectful to enlightened authority.

I took my answer, Jonathan's answer, to Sensei, who grunted and continued with further parts of the koan, to see if I had gotten the implications of Tokusan's detached behavior, but I answered in the same vein. He kept grunting consents. We passed on to the next koan.

Maybe Baba was right too. It could be that koans are overrated, but this particular riddle has stayed with me so far. Jonathan's answer is the solution to problems illustrated in gangster movies. All those spectacular gunfights become unnecessary when the dons realize their Tokusan nature. Applying the principle of practical submission would be the end of the arms industry. It has worked in my own life because my own personality seems particularly vulnerable when it has the idea that it "gets no respect around here." If I can find a quiet voice in myself to tell it it is okay, that Seppo is just another lout and what else is new in this world of boorish egotism but not to worry—lunch is still coming, it'll just be a little late—things usually turn out okay after all. Similar internal dialogues never fail to save the day. Older brother, the observer, tells younger brother, the doer, not to lose his cool;

after all, didn't the little fellow study Zen for a while? The toddler promptly simmers down and takes the dog for a walk instead of pounding the kitchen table and incurring wrath from stupidly slow cooks, which would surely have led to unnecessary trouble.

"What if Tokusan had yelled at Seppo?" I asked Jonathan.

"I'm sure, in reality, he did." He used his British stutter. "I s-s-say . . ." Jonathan the Natural said he thought that, in the actual and unedited scene, short-tempered sensei Tokusan probably had roared insults at uppity head monk Seppo before stamping back to his room, but reporting on everyday events accurately doesn't create usable koans. He winked at me. "Does it now, old chap?"

WHO THE HELL WAS BUDDHA?

My introduction to Zen was in the Japan of the late fifties, in the temple city of Kyoto. No pollution, no gridlock. Things were like they were supposed to be, as I innocently walked into my Far Eastern dream. The temple my karma took me to was Daitoku-ji, a vast Buddhist complex built long ago in an even more ancient style, that of T'ang Dynasty architecture copied from Chinese records. Sloping roofs swept up at the corners, plastered walls topped with slate tiles, statues of ego-destroying monsters guarding monumental gates, raked rock and gravel compositions, evergreen trees and bushes artfully cut, carefully maintained moss gardens, giant goldfish in shallow clear ponds, curved bridges—it was all there, the ideal background of monks and priests on *geta*, jazzy-sounding wooden clogs, and in simple robes, under shiny shaven heads. Seeing this mystical splendor, I stopped doubting whether I would find at least some answers.

Although Christianity, the faith of my youth, got wiped out by the atrocities of World War II—it's hard to believe in love when your schoolmates are kicked into cattle cars labeled for a death camp—I did hold on to the idea that if I wanted to make sense of a bewildering world all I had to do was "knock and the door will be opened." The gates of Daitoku-ji happened to be open when I arrived after a long and complicated journey three-quarters of the way around the world, but I knocked anyway. There was a huge copper bell, complete with wooden hammer, and I hit it. I felt like an actor in a classic Japanese movie. Were spiritual samurai going to come out to lead me to an enlightened master? I stood in awe. The booming sound of the huge bell brought out monks, who were in awe too, for that bell is only hit on important occasions. It wasn't New Year, there wasn't a forthcoming gathering of high Zen officials, it wasn't the Buddha's birthday; it was just me, a *gai-jin*, an outsider clamoring to be let into their superior and exclusive world. They would have liked to be rid of me there and then, but the abbot ignored their recommendations.

The auspicious event happened forty years ago, and I will always appreciate the teacher's decision. His small, immaculate human projection, with the kindly smile and the insightful slanting eyes under comically raised eyebrows, is still a visualization that helps me through trying moments. If there is such a phenomenon as a living deity, then surely Roshi was just that. When mental clouds gather I ask my memory of him to sit next to me, and I hear the rustle of his clean linen robe when he moves about to see where I've taken him this time. I never ask the memory for help; there is no need to try to shake his detachment. When alive he seemed very detached in his efforts, constantly dedicated to bringing about his pupils' inner freedom. He gave the impression of going all out without caring about any results. It helped, perhaps, that when I met him he knew he was close to his death. His official title was *roshi*, meaning "old man," and now that I am an old man myself, life's daily irritations lose their edges. Old age, especially when coupled with an awareness of a terminal disease, tends to naturally release us from Ego Big Mouth, even in a man who, during most of his life, is used to being respected and getting his wishes granted. In Roshi's case, personal concerns must have been minimal anyway. He never owned anything except a few robes, and he never seemed to attach importance to his title. Roshi, schmoshi. Who is there to care? His body suffered from a serious version of Parkinson's disease, but his shaking hands didn't keep him from helping out in the kitchen after long meditations and a strenuous series of active get-togethers with his students. Being on his way out, he had less reason to be concerned with the worldly advice of his senior monks. I was never more than a marginal student, not enthusiastic about being a diligent devotee, but the way he treated me showed that he accepted my motivation. I was, and am, kept afloat by the "great doubt," a philosophical affliction suffered by little kids, drunks, fools, schizophrenics. It is a curse to be unable to accept positive answers as to what's what. It isn't nice, either, to have no faith in a benevolent power creating a perfect universe. The disease had ripped me out of a comfortable existence. Nervously I knocked on the biblical door, which happened to be Buddhist, and a genuine Zen master, a guide on a path starting up when Buddha silently raised a flower to answer my question, did let me in.

Roshi treated me respectfully, accepting me as a genuine seeker. He joked around, too. One early morning, he climbed down from his cushions, prostrated his aching body in front of me, and addressed me as Jan-Buddha: "What, Jan-Buddha, are you looking so gloomy about?" At another occasion he laughed

and said, "You are like a fish in the ocean complaining of thirst."
He insisted that I already, in my true being, knew everything, was everything, was in need of nothing. "But I am in need of you giving me that 'nothing,' sir," I commented, remembering I had read that the Buddhist base is the Void, nothing. I thought I would like to experience that nothing. I wanted him to take me there. I liked that idea: aiming for, eventually reaching, total emptiness. It somehow made me think of Harley-Davidsons and naked women.

Roshi told me not to hold on to nothing, either.

"Be what you are already, Jan-Buddha—free, free even of nothing."

"Let go. Let go!" He tumbled about on his platform, letting go of emptiness too, looking exuberant, clapping his hands.

This is dangerous talk. Zen students, driven crazy by their teachers' urging to "let go," have stepped off bridges and buildings to jump into their deaths, but I think Roshi believed I wouldn't embarrass him by making a terminal spectacle of his disciple. "I'll see what I can do for you," I said. He thought that was funny. "Do some zazen for me, then show me your freedom. Let go, Jan-Buddha."

He taught on different levels. When I came, he asked me what I had done before I rang the bell at his open gate. I had told him I had made money. So why had I given up on that? "Money has no true substance, sir."

"But you do have money?" he asked, frowning furiously. He pointed at the kitchen's smoking chimney, at the cigarettes glowing on the ashtray between us, at the steaming teapot at his side. He told me what these insubstantial things cost in Japan. Firewood at Y200 a cord, Shinsei cigarettes at Y50 a pack of twenty, green tea, even the cheap ban-cha used at his temple, had just jumped to Y29 a metric ounce. Nothing cheap there. He couldn't have me live in the monks' quarters, the blessed *sodo*, for free. He was going to charge me big bucks for his trouble. He looked so anxious that I brought out my wallet and showed him a stack of traveler's checks. "Good, good." Roshi was much relieved. Later, when a monk came to my room to have me complete some paperwork, I saw that what I was supposed to pay for a month's board and lodging was what, according to the cab driver who had taken me to the temple, a reasonable man might spend for a night in the Red Quarter.

I did need money, Roshi assured me, and I did need to let go, even of my all-important nothing.

One of the monks told me while we were weeding a moss patch that he wanted nothing, and plenty of it. Mo-san was a good old boy when I met him, apparently not caring for anything much, not even about being very short of stature. Reputedly he made rapid progress in his koan study. Mo-san never worried about insect bites, long hours, poor food, drafts in the dining room, being ordered around by the head monk. I thought this supercool character would have an impeccable career. "Show you a trap and you fall into it," a monkey told a future sage whom he was accompanying on his path to the Buddhas temple, according to a Chinese legend (*Monkey*, by Wu Ch'eng-en, a sixteenth-century allegoric novel I was reading at the time). Mo-san's trap turned out to be his very "noncaring diligence." He did care about being selected to be a teaching priest in magic America. I heard that, some ten years later, he became a substitute master in an American Zen temple on the West Coast. During his tenure he hid his shortness by wearing platform soles under lengthened robes and insisted that his lay disciples buy him a Cadillac to glide about in. He evoked a scandal by trying to trade insights for intimate encounters with tall blondes, and I was told he handed in his teaching ticket. Mo-san must be old now. I'm sure he is doing just fine. Zen monks who have gotten into trouble and feel they have to make up often become successful hermits. When they leave the *sangha*, the Buddhist uniformed brotherhood, altogether, they usually do well at whatever comes with their next occupation. Putting up with painful and maddening meditations, thankless work in vegetable gardens, humility toward power-mad superiors, and going without often brings about a dauntless spirit that keeps going in the face of adversity.

An American ex–Zen monk, a powerful man with red hair that would glow within an hour after shaving his skull, became a model long-distance driver. We met again at a truck stop in northern Arizona. A man I once knew as brother Joe was meticulously mixing a soda at a multifaucet machine. One-third Coke, one-quarter Sprite, forty-one-percent iced tea, squirted in turns into his cup answering an experienced flick of the wrist, a measured pressure of the finger. "You still like the ceremonies?" I asked Joe while trying to get just enough mustard on hot dogs for my wife and myself. Joe said he liked doing nothing better than mixing the ultra-soda. "Compulsion didn't get me far in the temple, but it sure makes me a happy trucker."

What about the doubt of existence?

Joe shrugged.

What about the Great Doubt that moved men like Hakuin, Lo Pi, Jack Kerouac, Bodhidharma, and the occasional modern poet?

What doubt?

I pointed at the night sky behind the truck stop's windows.

What of it?

The questions raised by the immensity, the beauty, the music, the horror of all and everything.

Joe said he didn't know about all and everything, but he had heard about wondering about the gigantic illusion of the night sky, marveling at the powerful curve of the breasts of the *TV Guide* cover girl, being thrilled by the tragic cry of the loon, being shocked by the howling of the survivors of the latest massacre in a country you can fly to in a few hours, but none of that ever got him to become a monk. He was more after "feeling good." He felt good in the temple because of the predictable discipline: bells and clappers at exactly 3 A.M., breakfast precisely four hours later, the timely meditations, the rigid calendar of events. He liked to know where he stood within time and space. Why worry about a senseless universe as long as prevailing routines keep a moderate euphoria going at a regular rhythm? Being good at the business of causing and suffering no surprises now got him to run schedules at a sizable Zen center. He smiled and pounded his chest. "Feeling good forever." Then fate tried him. The abbot of Joe's meticulously run retreat got suddenly transferred. His successor, an Aquarian ruled by Uranus, the fickle planet of happenstance, a Korean master who liked to pull the mat out from under his pupils, called his administrator "Robot-san."

"It occurred to me," the born-again trucker told me, "that that was exactly what I wanted to be. A robot." He saluted. "By then I knew enough to be a robot on my own." He looked at my hot dog. "I still keep the precepts. No meat. You still meditate?"

"Not too often."

"I meditate in motel rooms." He was still saluting, but now dropped his hand. "On my own. Yessir, I quit that fickle foreigner's erratic meddling." He dropped his hand. "Doing good now. And how are *you* doing?"

"I wish I knew," I said.

Joe marched to the cabin of his eighteen-wheeler. The vertical exhausts belched flames, he waved, the immaculate rig rumbled off.

"How sad," my wife said, but I wasn't so sure. In fact I was jealous of Mr. Arizona Supertruck. The guy looked good in his matching jeans and jacket and hat. Muscular. Wide-chested. Joe evidently found time, in between customized sodas, to work out in roadside gyms while his obedient monster waited outside. "Keep on trucking."

"Keep on doubting," my wife said. "I rather prefer that in a man."

"There's a koan about this," I told my wife.

"Tell me," she said patiently.

It had to do with Manjusri, the bodhisattva of concentration, who lives as a statue on altars in zendos, and wields a sword to cut thoughts with. The bodhisattva explained *Mahaprajna*, the perfection of wisdom, saying, "The true practicer of austerities does not fly into nirvana. The monk who breaks the precepts does not slide into hell."

My wife was glad that I would not go to hell, but she was sorry to hear that Joe was missing nirvana. But then, after more hot dogs, she took that back. "Is there a downward and an upward way in Buddhism?"

I didn't think so.

"So you and Joe are both doing okay, doubting, trucking?"

I thought so.

"But are you a Buddhist?"

No, I was not. I had tried to become a Buddhist in 1960, when leaving Japan, and Roshi had confirmed that he could perform a ceremony to make it so, but did I think it would improve my chances if he put on his brocades and the monks performed on percussion and chanted?

I had asked him if he was a Buddhist, and he'd said he had no idea. He waved his hands in consternation and stamped his feet. He switched to the growling tones of street language used by bad guys in Japanese action movies. "Who the hell was Buddha anyway?" Then he laughed and slapped my shoulder "*Yosh*— Okay?"

SIXTY ZEN MASTERS
CAN'T BE WRONG

The priest Sekiso said, "You're on the top of a hundred-foot pole. Now, how do you advance?"

It's always nice to run into an example. It took me a while to accept that the monk addressing me in pure American with a cultured New England accent was a sixth-generation citizen of the United States, pure White-Anglo-Saxon-Protestant, with an ivy-university background. Harvard, my surprise visitor told me. Oriental studies. He could have fooled me; I was sure he was Japanese when he came clacking up our driveway in geta, robes, shaved head, the starched Zen bib (a square made of linen) dangling on his chest, a black attaché case clasped firmly in a suntanned hand. He had all the Japanese mannerisms. If you asked him something he wasn't sure about or didn't care to comment on, he kept his head to the side and said "Saaaa . . ." If he was irritated, he *tsk*ed in oriental fashion, reminding me of the grackles when I had forgotten to fill the bird feeder: "*Tsk-tsk*, someone being negligent again." Bobbie-san hissed his appreciations, like the monks in the Kyoto sodo, when a kind old lady had brought in a bucket of hot *udon*, Japanese noodles, with side dishes in plastic containers, "*Sssss, oishiiiii*—tasty." He recognized, responded to, and practiced perfectly the thousand-and-one different Japanese bows. He did have green eyes. I had never seen a Japanese with green eyes. Maybe a Caucasian grandmother? Bobbie-san finally convinced me that he had four Caucasian grandmothers, really, absolutely all-American, was a former high-school basketball star, a connoisseur of hamburgers, a knowledgeable differentiator between Coke and Pepsi, the son of a CEO of a well-known corporation headquartered in Boston.

"Welcome," I said. I am very fond of Americans. They liberated Holland from the Nazis; I'm glad they allow me to live in their vast and beautiful country. Bobbie-san smiled. He said he came to bring me a pair of straw sandals and greetings from a distant relative I had worked with once.

Bobbie-san stayed in my studio for a while. I was elated. Here was what I had longed to become long ago, a fully trained, fully enlightened, bilingual, bicultured Western Zen monk. My hero. Maitreya himself, the legendary future Buddha. Supposedly, according to Sakyamuni Buddha, the former Indian prince of two and a half millennia ago, Maitreya will be next in line to try to save the persistently ignorant human species. Maitreya Buddha, it was noted, is to project his pure being into the body of a white man from the West. One statue of Maitreya I saw in Kyoto showed the future knower (the verb *budh* means "to know") as a Viking, blond, blue-eyed, with a stern demeanor. Bobbie-san still looked like a Japanese with green eyes to me, but this was just another aspect of a miracle on my doorstep. I was so excited I stuttered to my wife when I introduced the remarkable being. Sage Bobbie-san from Boston and Nagasaki. "Look what we've got here, dear," I shouted at my wife.

We ate noodles with clam sauce that night, slurping away in true Japanese fashion, burping in unison when the meal was over, a most remarkable meal, for Bobbie-san had made a seaweed salad from greens picked from my own shoreland. Here I had all these delicious water plants growing for free around my dock and I never knew that, either. I felt sure I was about to make a quantum leap, both in body and mind. A mystical dream come true.

"Show you a trap," Monkey told his master, the legendary Chinese monk who was painfully struggling to complete his journey to the Buddha's paradise in the old days, "and you'll jump into it." The monk gagged Monkey for his troubles, using his semi-enlightened magic. He put a bandana around the animal's head that caused a splitting headache if the monk recited a mantra. I had done that too. The critical part of mind was never popular with me. Listen here, Bobbie-san had completed his koan study, had done his umpteen years in sodo and zendo training, had weathered all upheavals the tough Nagasaki zendo had devised to test his endurance, insight, egolessness, so why doubt any of this magnificent status?

It took a few days of chopping wood in my backyard, fertilizing the broccoli patch, harvesting mussels on the shore of the cove my land overlooks, discussing the finer points of Maitreya's mission, before Bobbie-san jumped up from his cushion, one quiet evening in front of the fireplace where three sticks of "summer wood" (which is what Mainers call alder) burned spectacularly, shook me by the shoulders, looked into my eyes, and whispered fiercely, "It's all bullshit, you fool!"

Huh? Maitreya had gone mad? Or was this Nagasaki Zen,

some fierce way of expressing the invalidity of the creation? "Bullshit as in 'samsara'?" I asked. "As in 'opposite of nirvana'?"

He went to bed after excusing himself. Too much bourbon on the rocks. He wasn't used to hard liquor.

The next day, when we were out rowing on the bay, he told me about his teacher, a famous roshi whom he accompanied to a Tokyo Zen-master convention. "These days," Bobbie said, "any self-respecting Zen teacher has to have his white discipline. Americans are particularly popular. I think it's like the Japanese want to win the war once and for all this time. Militarily they lost and economically they seem to be overreaching themselves now perhaps, but spiritually they will conquer the ignorance of the rest of the world. By training White disciples, Japanese Zen, will finally shed its pure light—the world will rejoice, and be grateful. Japanese superiority will be respectfully acknowledged. The next space program will be Japanese led. Japanese Zen will fill space. The universe will bow, say Hai, and serve sushi."

"Whoa." I suggested we get back to basics. Zen is not typically Japanese. The Buddha was an Indian. He held up a rose when a monk inquired about life's meaning. Holding the rose, Buddha quietly left the stage. Nobody understood what Buddha, "He Who Knows," meant except one advanced disciple, an Indian like the Buddha himself.

Bodhidharma became the first *dhyana* ("meditation") master. He was a teacher of the silent school, which would eventually crystallize into a system using zazen, sanzen, and koans. He became a missionary in China. Next we get all the Chinese ch'an masters (dhyana was translated into Chinese as "ch'an"), spearheaded by Tokusan of the bowl, Joshu of the puppy dog, Gozo of the tail of the bull, Sekiso of the hundred-foot pole. Hakuin, who drew cartoons of himself while sitting behind a big folded belly, was a Japanese Zen master (ch'an was called Zen in Japan), but he came much later.

"Besides," I protested, "linking insight to a nationality or a race is silly. Pure being is everywhere, even in me, and I am Dutch, for God's sake. Can you imagine?"

Bobbie-san said he probably couldn't imagine a Dutch Buddha, but why try? The Japanese contemporary point was that only Japanese masters know the meaning of nonmeaning, the sound of silence, and the location of the mustard jar that Abraham found. However, these masters were willing to share. They were passing their enlightenment to Bobbies. It was a Buddhist new-age thing, this insistence on having a white disciple. It was a fad, Bobbie claimed. He, Bobbie, had been declared to be the most perfect white disciple around, which gave his teacher a lot of face. Bobbie, Harvard graduate, who came with an IQ in the high hundreds, had picked up Japanese so well that Nagasaki folks thought he was one of them and summoned their protective spirits when they were told he was a green-eyed demon. "You know how many kan-ji, Japanese characters, I know" Bobbie-san asked me. "No? All of them. You know how many sutras, Buddhist scripture, I can chant in formalized classic Chinese? All of them, too. You know how much lay folks pay to have me perform the rites at their home altars? Up to a thousand dollars."

He made me think of the man at the top of the pole, another koan that Sensei had me break my brain on. Top of the pole, but I hadn't got there yet. Bobbie-san evidently had. His teacher kept telling him "You're there, you've done it, but you're too young. You have to be my private attendant, hang out with me, learn the practice now that you have the theory—soon I'll launch you on your career." Top of the pole? Some famous commentary says, "Take the next step." That's what I finally came up with too. Who wants to be on top of a hundred-foot pole anyway, with the point sticking up one's ass? Keep moving. All that enlightenment to balance on, away with it. Keep going, then fall or fly. "Did you fall or fly?" I asked my guest, who was leaning on his oars. We were floating toward a ledge where seals anxiously shuffled about, waiting for the all-enlightened answer.

Bobbie-san never heard me. "We went to the Zen congress. There was a lot of confusion; trains and planes had been delayed by driving rain and thunderstorms. We, the acolytes, were carrying bags and showing off our detachment to each other. So we were late, so what. The teachers were trying to stay calm too, but they were concerned about having a bath, getting into their brocade robes, their starched white socks, their calligraphed enlightenment bibs, which might all have gotten crumpled in their cases. The roshis were hungry, irritable, tired. Monastic life is orderly. The master is king—he flicks his fingers and his favorite tofu soup appears, white rice on one side, assorted pickles on the other. Here they had to deal with modern foods, chips, nuts, Western-style processed snacks that came with complimentary soda, served while they were waiting to check in. The hotel was disorderly, staff members were beside themselves, trying to figure out which master was holier than whom. There is good karma in serving holy men; where would the servants rush to barter their services for good karma? Some of the masters were famous—they showed up regularly on TV—but here in the hotel one bald old monk looked much like another. 'Who is Suzuki roshi from Kobe?' stewards and chambermaids asked us, the attendants, in tactful whispers. 'Who is Yamaha roshi from Yokohama?' Some tried to tip us. Some of us accepted the tips."

"Jesus." I laughed.

"Jesus on the steps of the temple," Bobbie-san said, "getting short-tempered with the merchants. I felt like that."

"You had money anyway, a thousand dollars a sutra chanting."

"Right." He nodded. "The hotel people were paying ten bucks or so."

Behind him seals slid off their shoals. Soon they surrounded our dory, looking at us with popping eyes. "*Then* what happened?"

What happened was that the roshis, frightened by the present chaos, all longed for the security of their home temples, simultaneously. They wanted to make contact with their home base, to make sure it was still there. Sleeves flapping, sandals slipping, the roshis rushed the phones in the hotel's lobby. The phones weren't working right, perhaps because of the heavy rainstorms and all the lightning, or because of a nervous operator. The malfunction caused all the roshis to be connected to all the wrong home temples. They were talking to monks with names and voices they had never heard of. "*Moshi moshi*—hello hello" the maddened teachers were shouting at noncomprehending parties who, in desperation, hung up. The roshis dialed again, and got through to other wrong monks. "*Moshi moshi*."

"That's funny." I said.

Bobbie-san didn't think so. The ordeal of having to watch sixty out-of-control holy folks had broken his spirit. He had a nervous breakdown and the hotel's doctor administered an opium derivative to stop his body from shaking. "I was out of it for the duration of the congress. Passed out in the roshi's room."

"You got pushed off a hundred-foot pole," I said.

"By whom?"

"By yourself?"

Bobbie-san thought that was very likely. He quoted Carl Jung. Insanity helps us to find our true being. It stops us from pursuing the wrong way. Rowing back, we explored the possibility of setting ourselves up for disaster so that we can break a bad routine. "I am good," Bobbie-san said. "I excel at my studies. Good brain. A pushy mind. Having the chance to study Zen in Japan after learning Japanese and Chinese culture in this country gave me a chance to add approved mysticism to a solid degree, but did I really want that?"

"What would you want?"

We both looked at the sunset between the Cleavage Mountains on Mount Desert Island. A most mysterious light touched the gigantic stone split. "You think I want the real thing?" Bobbie-san asked. "True insight? Of course I do."

His teacher insisted that Bobbie-san had found the real thing. Fifty-nine other Zen teachers backed up the verdict. Sixty Zen masters have got to be right. They had all walked the way themselves. Finish koan study and the pupil is done and only needs to be confirmed as a master. A mere formality that Bobbie-san's teacher would perform in due time. What was this sudden doubting? So Bobbie-san had a bit of an upset in the Tokyo hotel— happens to the best of saints. Listen to your betters. Stick with tradition. Wear your Zen bib and shave your skull. Chant the sutras.

"At a thousand dollars a clip," I said.

Well-paying profession. Bobbie-san said that one of the sixty teachers used a white Rolls-Royce to impress his audience at weddings and cremations. The car had been donated by a constituent who sold uniforms to the Japanese Imperial Army. The roshi also drove it to his city's Willow Quarter, where courtesans and restaurateurs bowed when they saw it gliding through their alleys.

I told him I had really liked the Kyoto Willow Quarter. "But later you quit all that," Bobbie-san said. "Carousing no longer fulfilled your needs so you got your wife to yell at you and you quit, right? By getting married you created a crisis that significantly changed the direction of your path. In Tokyo I created my crisis. Sixty clowns proved that I had to jump off my pole."

"So what are you doing now?" I asked my guest.

Bobbie-san had been asked to leave the temple when he'd refused to be confirmed as a teacher to be sent into the world with the blessing of his master. He was traveling now. Checking things out. Looking at options. He was thinking of doing some translation work when he got back to Japan. Maybe he would also start a vegetable garden. He had been asked to take care of a small temple outside Nagasaki. There are many empty small temples in Japan. As they are potential tourist attractions and, possibly, therapeutical to stress-related diseases, city governments like to finance qualified priests to have buildings repaired and gardens restored. "I will chant the Heart Sutra every morning," Bobbie told me. "It will help me to rely on nothing."

I took Bobbie-san over to Ben-san's pagoda. Ben-san had gotten himself a dog, a puppy with large ears that it kept stepping on. My habitually moody friend seemed a changed man, smiling, eager to please, offering more homebaked biscuits with generic orange marmalade. "This dog truly has some Buddha nature," Ben told Bobbie. "First appreciative company I ever had. We have a good time together. Once his legs grow and his ears get off the ground we're going to go hiking together."

Walking the ten-mile path back to the town of Sorry, Bobbie-san said he might grow his hair and dress in jeans and a jacket for a while. Zen priests can do that when they feel they need a different experience "to flesh out their insights." Zen priests aren't sworn to celibacy, either. Bobbie planned to rent a Toyota Land Cruiser for his sabbatical, tour Japan, stay at inns, look around, meet some women.

I suddenly felt tired and had to sit on a log for a while.

Bobbie paced in front of me. "Yes. I have been told sex is easy in Japan. No stigma, yes?"

"Not when I was there," I told him. "Girls threw rocks into the sodo's courtyard with invitations attached with red ribbons. Monks climbed the walls at night. I once got a rock on my head. Fortunately I had thick hair, never shaved it. I always was a layman."

Bobbie-san was still pacing. "Same in Nagasaki, girls asking me out, but I was too busy. Perfecting my knowledge of the language. There was always koan study, meditations, escorting the abbot, chores." He nodded a few times, very quickly, putting strain on his neck muscles. "Well, I plan to find out."

I guessed his age. "You must be over forty? You never . . ."

"Not yet," Bobbie-san said nervously. "But I'm going to rent that Cruiser. Stay at comfortable inns here and there. I have some savings. Maybe I meet somebody. I can spend a while trying. Nothing serious, of course."

"There are quite a few words for 'paid female companion' in Japanese," I said, getting up from the log. "You must have come across the terminology in your studies."

"Fifty-six different kinds of prostitutes," Bobbie-san said. "Should be interesting to explore the different levels. As I said, I do have some savings. And time. I do plan to rent that Cruiser. I'm getting my driving license. Should be helpful. Get away from Manjusri, the disciplinary deity, embrace Kwannon, goddess of compassion. Take the next step. Get off my hundred-foot pole. What do you think?"

Joshu and the Old Woman

A koan that particularly annoyed me, especially coming from Sensei, who was never interested in women, was the old-woman riddle. My frustration eventually helped me solve the koan that featured Joshu, the priest in the Mu koan where he tells a monk that a puppy gamboling about their feet does not (*mu*) have Buddha nature (*bussho*). On another occasion he is supposed to have told a monk that yes (*u*), surely, of course, the puppy does have Buddha nature. Back in Japan I was, after a trial period of three months, given the Mu koan by Roshi, who made me write down the Chinese characters wording the riddle and insisted that I would recite the koan in the strange classical no-longer-spoken Chinese that Japanese Zen monks use for their holy texts. I still recite that koan from time to time, when life particularly puzzles me, and the little singsong is always comforting: *Joshu, osho, chinami ni, so, to, kushi, ni, kaette, Bussho, ari ya, mata, inai ya, Joshu, iwaku, Mu, U:*

> *Joshu* (his name)
> *osho* (his rank, "priest")
> *chinami ni* (toward, someone is coming to him)
> *so* (monk)
> *to* (inquires)
> *kushi* (puppy dog)
> *ni* (about, something about the puppy dog)
> *kaette* (perhaps)
> *Bussho* (Buddha nature)
> *ari ya* (does have?)
> *mata* (or)
> *inai ya* (does not have?)
> *Joshu* (the priest's name)
> *iwaku* (answers)
> *Mu* (*not*, no, nothing, the void, total absence)

And when asked again, Joshu answers U (yes, everything, totally). Which makes perfect sense, for *samsara* (the illusion) is *nirvana* (blissful extinction). I'm not writing this and you're not reading this. Nothing ever happened.

Nothing matters. There is no tomorrow; yesterday didn't occur. Whoever gets this basic truth can sit at the side of the road, like the Chinese "laughing Buddha," often shown in restaurants as a fat happy figure, and be amused while a war rages right in front of his eyes, while children starve and dogs are beaten. Sometimes I think I get it, but even while under the illusion of realizing my Buddha nature as prompted by the koan's hint I would try to free the dogs and fly them, and the hungry kids too, of course, to Hawaii in a stolen war plane. Or not, most likely. Bewildered by the complexity of the plane's dashboard, I would be caught by the Anti-Joy Police and shot at dawn, after reciting the koan. *"Joshu osho chinami ni so to kushi ni kaette Bussho ari ya mata inai ya? Yoshu iwaku mu."* "What are you saying?" the officer commanding the firing squad would yell. "It means *fuck you*, sir, in classical Chinese used by Japanese Zen monks, something I picked up on my travels." "Oh, very well," the officer would yell, raising his baton. "Men? Are you ready? Uh-one, uh-two . . ."

This very same priest Joshu, a historical figure whose Chinese name was Chaochou, lived, as physically as you and I today, from 778 through most of 897, making him almost 120 years old when he was finally done with prodding the unenlightened along. The factual information I mentioned here comes from the British Buddhist scholar Dr. Reginald Horace Blyth (1898–1968), a controversial Zen "adept" who lived in Japan, was interned there during the war, and later became tutor to the Japanese crown prince. An American Zen priest whom I met in Japan, where he was the priest in charge of a beautiful little Daitoku-ji subtemple, restored at his private expense, told me, "Blyth talked too much—the man should have been throttled at birth," but that, no doubt, was Zen talk, intended to shock me into some awareness. Blyth was close to the famous Japanese Zen scholar Dr. D. T. Suzuki, who also wrote widely on Zen and was the first "Zen man" to do so in English.

Dr. Blyth, in Volume Four of his *Zen and Zen Classics* (Hokuseido Press, first printing 1966), has Joshu be a student of Nansen, who was only ten generations away from the first Zen master in China, the Indian Daruma, also known as Bodhidharma. We are very close to the beginning here. Zen patriarch Nansen died in 834, when Joshu was fifty-seven. After that Joshu visited all the famous Zen teachers in China; the journey took him twenty years. Finally knowing enough at age eighty, he became the abbot of a temple dedicated to the bodhisattva of compassion, a female deity, called Kwan-Yin, Kwannon in Japanese. Out of this temple, Kwannon-in, he taught. The puppy and the inquiring monk appeared. Joshu became famous for saying "When a sincere man teaches a wrong doctrine the doctrine becomes truth: when an insincere man expounds a true doctrine it becomes error."

True enough, but what concerns me here is Joshu's attitude toward the old woman, the koan I struggled with for so long. The background of the riddle is that a woman, who probably wasn't old at all but became old because she insulted some monks who then referred to her as "old woman" (old-fashioned Buddhism being chauvinistic), ran a tea shop on the road to a famous Chinese mountain. The mountain, of course, is still there, and called Sumeru, or Taizan, "big mountain," and even today there are monasteries and lamaseries there. Mount Sumeru is symbolic for enlightenment, the ultimate teaching; it is as huge and solid as the dharma, the Buddhist teaching itself. Here is the koan:

> A traveling monk asks the old woman "Which way to Mount Sumeru," she says "straight ahead," he goes straight ahead, and she sneers at his back, saying, "This fine monk goes the same way." The monk, feeling insulted, complains to his teacher Joshu. Joshu says he'll check the old woman out. He visits the tea shop, asks for the way to Sumeru, is told to go straight ahead, the story repeats itself. Joshu returns to his temple and tells his monks, "The old woman has been penetrated by me."

Penetrated! Even Sensei did not deny the sexual implication. Surely the Buddhist priest didn't run some kind of deadly weapon through a cheeky lady running a tea shop. I twisted and turned with the tale for several training sessions. Often Sensei rang his bell as I came into the sanzen room; I hadn't even had time to prostrate myself in front of his throne. "Out with you, stupid."

Out I went, carrying a ninety-year-old man having sex with a wrinkled old tea lady, and what for? Why were Joshu, and the monks before him, asking for the way to one of China's highest mountains, anyway? Were these highly trained folks blind? Good thing the tea lady laughed at them. "Straight ahead, sirs, you can't miss it—it's over there, poking its peak into the clouds. See it?" The monks march along, *one two, one two*. The woman laughs behinds their backs. "This fine monk goes the same way." Then the petty fellows go back to their home temple to complain to Big Daddy, and then Joshu himself picks up his gnarled stick, and has a cup of tea with the lady after she tells him "It's in front of your nose, dear," and they have such a good time together that he spends the night with her. Joshu lived to tell his students about it. "The old woman has been penetrated by me."

Was there ginseng in the tea? Powdered rhinoceros horn?

This is a weird tale and I solved it by shouting into Sensei's face: "Silly old monk, silly old woman." I thumbed my nose at Sensei to make quite sure. He said, "Okay okay, let's pass to the next one. It's okay. Calm down now. You're not showing insight, you know—you're just mad." I was, and it was the right answer.

Surely we know what is going on by now. How many times have we reincarnated and we still don't get it? "Where is Mount Enlightenment?" "Straight ahead, dear." Do we keep going? Get on with our lives? Make the best use of any given set of circumstances that happens to come along? No, we sit, fret, desperately look for a confirmation that, apart from marching straight ahead, our ego-existence is of some value. What could that value be except nothing? Whatever our personalities may think they are achieving will come to nothing. The very earth we stand on will disappear. One day (but what kind of a day is a day when the sun no longer rises?), one moment (what kind of a moment when we have nothing to keep time with?) there will be no planet to call our own. There were other days when there was no Earth, because it hadn't been born yet. After it dies, as it will, as it will, there'll be just empty space where it, and we on it, used to be. Imagine a couple of future personalities in their spaceship traversing the space where the Earth once materialized on its way around a sun, which has meanwhile gone too, for stars don't last either. Would the one being say to the other, in between checking dials on the dashboard, "Hey, Sputmack my pal, Earth used to be here—did you *know* that?" Now what kind of question is that? Of course Sputmack wouldn't know that the emptiness passing by the craft's windows at a speed of nearly multi-Mach 17 was once filled with a view of a planet that some forgotten race of extinct creatures called "Earth." There are zillions of disappeared planets—is poor Sputmack supposed to remember them all? Or any? And if he wanted to remember, because he was a student of history, what would make him select Earth and its painful past of egotistic misery ended by a technology handled by dimwits? No, that spacecraft would just keep zipping along and the two pilots would be blissfully unaware of a cry of terror that played itself out an eon ago.

How to get to the point where we can accept the unimportance of our empty egos? By going straight along, without bothering tea ladies.

While in Japan, trying to penetrate this kind of problem, I had a helpful dream. The monks practicing at Daitoku-ji sodo at that time were mostly either farmers' sons, given to the temple because their parents were glad to get rid of a hungry mouth, or sons of village priests destined to take over their fathers' temples. They hadn't been schooled on worldly matters too well. The year was 1958, and Japan was still poor, rebuilding the infrastructure wiped out by World War II. Recent history was humiliating, and boys who fantasized about being samurai wielding swords while serving mythical masters and having affairs with high-class courtesans didn't want to look at maps showing countries breeding foreign devils who had gotten away, for a while, with Japanese glory. They were willing to accept that there was America and Europe, but no one had ever heard of Holland. The Dutch Indies? Where were they? A Dutch war fleet that had fought the Japanese? Dutch? What is Dutch? Dutch soldiers in Japanese camps? Dutch civilians in Japanese camps? They had died there? No kidding. I thought of telling my spiritual colleagues in the sodo about the island of Deshima, where early-nineteenth-century Dutch merchants and scholars had lived close to the Japanese coast, trading and teaching. I wanted to remind them of many Japanese words of Dutch origin. But why bother? Well, because this touched my own identity. If Holland was nothing to them, then I was nothing to them, nothing but a performing bear put in their sodo to amuse them. Who cares what woods the circus bear was caught in? Watch him dance in pain. Can't cross his legs in the zendo. Got four limbs and a head, but he sure isn't human. Look at his long toes. They curl over the geta. Can't get geta the size of this monster's feet. Watch him loosen his mouth's lining when he chews on a salted plum. Most entertaining.

Then there was the dream. I was taking part in a meeting of beings. The being next to me wanted to be polite. It asked where I was from. I said I was from Earth. "How *interesting*," the being said, but it clearly had no idea where "Earth" could be. So I explained. "Milky Way Galaxy?" The being still had no idea. "Universe?" Nope. Nothing. I had no identity; I was from nowhere. In the dream I felt relieved. Nothing to carry, nothing to worry about. I didn't really want to come back to my aching body wrapped in a futon that mice had been at again, digging holes to mine the fluffy cotton they used for their own nests.

At that time I didn't have enough Japanese to tell Roshi what I had been dreaming, but perhaps he knew, for the morning afterward, when I came in at three-thirty, he patted my shoulder with his stick and said, "Good." I did tell Han-san, the only

English-speaking monk in the sodo, but he thought the dream was self-evident, kicking in an open door. He showed what he meant by sliding the papered door of my room to the side and trying to kick a hole in thin air. "Nothing doing," he said, winking.

Han-san also told me about Joshu, as he knew I was working on the priest and the puppy dog. "Joshu did other things too, you know." "Like what?" "Like playing *pam-pam* with old women." Pam-pam was what the monks called the Western-type sandwiches I sometimes prepared in my room. The way the sliced bread got cut, buttered, and smacked together reminded them of what they went after when they climbed the temple's walls at night, dressed in suits and hats, armed with money they had gotten from Mom in the mail, or the pittance the head monk handed out once in a while. Pam-pam. Hey hey!

"Joshu Osho did that?" I asked Han-san. Han-san was a fairly high-ranking monk. I hadn't heard him being blasphemous before. Joshu? The oldest man in Zen? He who devised the opening koan, the great gate? The patriarch of patriarchs? What was Han-san saying?

"Sure," Han-san said, patting me down to see if I had any cigarettes so he could bum one, "pam-pam, with some old mountain lady—the old boy just loved it."

THEN CARRY IT ALONG

"Then carry your gloom along," the master says, and off the disciple slinks, back into a heavy world. We were doing a lot of that in the hermitage, Sensei's place. I remember an attractive woman who, in a matter of months, became ugly at the hermitage: bent over, always dressed in a dirty raincoat, mumbling to herself. If she wasn't cleaning Sensei's kitchen she was killing and cutting up chickens. She also meditated early mornings and late nights. She would became enraged when she was disturbed at her after-lunch half-hour nap. "This is my only time of rest. Switch off the goddamn record player—right now." "But I'm listening through my phones." "Never mind, I can hear it squeaking." Students were spying on each other. "Sensei, Seeing-into-his-

Nature (advanced students had holy names), hasn't been doing zazen on his own for weeks. He says he's doing Full Lotus on the moon rock in the moss garden, but he keeps sneaking off to the haystack to take naps." Other students were just depressed. Whatever you said to them, they would answer by mumbling a slow "Hai!" That's Japanese for yes, but, linguistically just indicates "I'm here." "Hai hai," the waitress says, but that doesn't mean you get more soup. It means you get what's on the menu, but she won't argue with you. "Hai hai, mister, whatever you say. I'm here. Doing my thing. Till quitting time. Not one second longer."

There must have been a time when Zen study was fun. While in Japan I kept hearing about two Chinese winos who, holding hands, ran about the slopes of Sumeru, the insight mountain mentioned before, wrote way-out poetry on birch bark, and stuck out their tongues at passers-by. Everybody loved them and left out choice food in forest glades so that the self-realized hop-alongs could fetch it at their leisure. There are other uplifting mythical images. Like the Zen poet followed by a servant carrying his liquor supply for the day and a spade, the spade to be used to dig a grave with in case the master doesn't survive his next adventure. Anybody who approached the cheerful seer was given an all-enlightened poem on the spot. The man was a national treasure and the emperor's third concubine stripped for him in the moonlight.

Antique Zen masters and their disciples were always hiking along nature paths, exchanging spiritual in-talk and laughing while they slapped each other's cheeks to illustrate a subtle point. If pupil, or even master, still lacked some minor insight, needed a little polishing of his spirit, the wanted article would be provided with the next resounding slap. Whatever happened, famine, pestilence, new taxes, conscription for the next civil war, all Zenners had a great sense of humor. Fear, in Zen students, was unheard of. Thinking nothing of their careers, futures, possessions, wives or sweethearts, offspring, aged parents, spiritual status, Zen folks would go all out to do the best they could think of under any circumstances, and be unconcerned about any results. Let the dice roll and come up with whatever numbers, all my predecessors would do is make optimal use of the figures given. Nothing was holy, Buddha was a shitstick,* and this universe just another joke. Get out there and play good jazz.

Whatever happened to these amusing fellows?

Why would Sensei gather us together to spread gloom over the congregation? He always expected just a little more, whatever we did and however we did it. The result was misery and strife. Disciples bit each other's backs. There was jockeying for positions. The disciples less-criticized than others became Sensei's dogs and sycophants, walking solemnly behind him to carry his cushions and alcohol on a tray. Alcohol, wisdom soup—we didn't drink the quality Sensei reserved for himself, but he would let us pour second grade, to soak a bunch of old koans in, so we could gum on them in a sad stupor (I can't remember ever having been happily drunk at his parties).

Is there no originality left? Must every new Zen master of the last thousand years (with the exception of Hakuin, whose off-the-wall presence lightens up the sect) carefully select a collection of well-used, dog-eared, chewed-and-spat-out sayings from the worn-out past? Is he then expected to bundle his choices and use them as his own original tool for prying loose the innards of his hapless students? Can't he think of his own anecdotes? Re-create incidents of his own past? From what I have seen in Western modern Zen schools, originality is frowned on. Slide along the groove or get kicked down the steps of the sanzen house. No

---

*A monk asked Master Ummon (862–949), "What is Buddha?" Ummon answered, "Buddha is a shitstick." These were pre–toilet paper days; people used sticks.

criticism of Sensei. Your guru is infallible. Tested. Found perfect. Didn't he spend his formative years in the uncheckable Far East? Can't he decipher ancient symbolic scripts? Haven't you heard him recite sutras? Isn't he so sublimely advanced that, since that evening when he was snoring in the zendo and fell over sideways in his sleep, it was decided, by no less an authority than Sensei, that he didn't need to sit with the flock anymore? Never mind that nothing he does ever seems to work out, that his star pupils are always leaving, that the buildings crumble, that the plumbing gets choked up, that loans are solicited but never paid, that the potatoes are shriveled, the raccoons keep raiding the chicken houses. Seek your salvation with diligence and make sure there is no partying after hours. Displease Sensei and sit extra hours in the other zendo that has no heat. Be sorry and sad. Work on your preprocessed koan. Take heart. You will pass to the next one sometime soon maybe, even if it is just because both teacher and pupil get bored by the seemingly everlasting misunderstandings. Clean one up and there is another. There are only a hundred and forty-four koans in the book and we don't want to let you off the hook too quickly. No, Joshu didn't mean quite this; he meant more a little like that, no, your answer is too contrived, ah, missed it again, you want me to hit you? Let's see if you know what "not a single thing is." The teacher yawns and picks his teeth, the student looks at a loose straw in the floor mat. Eventually he will repeat what Sensei has just told him, or act out what Sensei just acted out. There is a great sigh of relief from the throne above him. "Okay, that's it. You passed. Next koan."

Pass a koan that way and you'll be bored with it forever. You don't want to even be reminded of the damned thing. Maybe there is a little virtue in the method, however, and some koans will, at least in my experience, come up again in unexpected circumstances, and may finally clear up just a tad of ignorance or stubborn denial. The carry-it-along koan didn't do much for me when I was reluctantly dragged through its many contortions, but it did show up later, and made an impression.

Having dealt with so many of my fellow beings during my travels and trades, I prided myself on my acute insight into the psyches of others. Zen masters are supposedly able to analyze their students, companions, and opponents at a single glance. A little helping of that sublime gift should have come my way, too. If it hadn't, what had I been wasting so much time on?

I got into a half-filled plane in Amsterdam once and saw an old lady sitting at a window. She wore the decent well-made everlasting clothes that I associated with high school teachers who specialized in making interesting subjects tedious, her hair was done up in a meticulous knot like long-gone Aunt Anna's (she sang very loudly in church), and she had put a large, square, efficient-looking handbag on the seat next to her that probably contained exhaustive files on irrelevant subjects. We made perfunctory eye contact. We said noncommittal "Hi"s. We deleted each other from memory. I sat in the window seat in front of her and read, tried to listen to Ornette Coleman on my CD player, and eventually fell asleep.

I woke up because the lady behind me shook my shoulder. She pointed out the window. "I thought you wouldn't want to sleep through this."

We flew over the coast of Greenland. It was late afternoon. Sunrays slanted at an angle. Below me luminous giant green rocks, frozen, mirroring each other, rose between bays filled with ice-blue water. There seemed to be no end to the jagged coastline. The odd shapes never repeated each other, each rocky promontory jagged in different semitransparent splendor. There were no trees, houses, roads, harbors. There were definitely no people. The empty landscape reminded me of an Escher composition, one that wouldn't end, recognized no limits, projected itself into an infinity of space. I kept looking until the winter light failed. I thanked the lady behind me. She invited me over to the seat next to her. We had airline-dinner together, which thanks to our togetherness, didn't taste bad at all. "Isn't the Earth beautiful?" she asked. "Divine mathematics, don't you agree? It's a poetic discipline. I'm fascinated by random shapes, also when they are expressed into figures. That undulating coast was like the movements of the stock market, random curves."

"You play the numbers?" I asked.

"Mornings only," she said. "In the afternoon I paint. I'm an afternoon artist."

"You sell your art?"

"Sometimes. I do abstract collages. My work is collectible, but I make more money on the market. And you?"

I gave her my card. She recognized my name. She had a friend who had read a book by me. "On Buddhism, right? *The Broken Mirror*? You went to Japan to figure things out? A funny tale? Wasn't it some book club's second choice once? You're still working in that direction?"

I told her I had dropped out of the official proceedings and her comments were cut off by the airline movie appearing on a screen ahead. A beautiful woman and her family were rafting down a fast river in what looked like rather a flimsy dingy while threatened by foamy waves and gunmen. Fortunately all ended well, for the beautiful woman anyway, but there were scary moments. Still shaken by the beautiful woman's ordeal, my companion asked me if I still "practiced Zen" on my own. It's the sort of question that makes me feel immediately guilty. Have I done my daily meditations? Do I walk the holy eightfold path? Do I think dirty? Do I eat dead cow? Yes ma'am, my mind is a brothel and I'm fond of large T-bone steaks, medium rare, with perished fried taters on the side, and murdered salad leaves that a cruel harvester pulled out of the ground, ignoring the painful squeaking of a tortured lettuce about to be robbed of its wonderful life. I take antibiotics to kill bacteria. I squash carpenter ants invading my house and if that doesn't help I feed them poison or spray them with killing fluid. I am aimed straight for all Dutch Reformed Buddhist hells. So what? I told my tormentor what the bodhisattva Avalokitasavara told his friend when he came back from "coursing in the deep prajnaparamita," cruising deep understanding. He said that he perceived that all five skandas are empty, thereby transcending all suffering. "That's nice," my fellow passenger said, "what are *skandas*?" Skandas are ego levels, I told her. That what makes up our awareness of self, like body, perception, consciousness, action, knowledge, all ultimately empty. Nothing to be worried about. Nothing to worry yourself with. Like the Maine saying. "If you don't give a shit," my neighbor in Maine tells me, "it don't matter." But then he also says, "Don't mean you ain't gotta do it."

She laughed. Dealing with the stock market in the morning and creating art works in the afternoon had given her a sense of relativity. Up and down, down and up. Worlds of bobbing values. Stocks diving and surging. Her art patrons loving her one day, ignoring her another. Her taste in her own art never the same. All these movements, why put value on them? Just keep making the moves, following the moves, but she thought she would give up on stock-market speculation soon and transfer her money into something boring, so that she could do more art, which she would probably destroy, for she could sell only a little and was running out of wall space. Maybe, she thought, she would take up meditation. She was moving to Santa Barbara, California, and she had heard there was a Hindu temple there, with quiet gardens. Dedicated to Ramakrishna, a saint. Had I heard of Ramakrishna? Who was in love with the goddess Kali, and cut off her head while, in a sublimely erotic vision, she was sleeping in his arms, after spiritual lovemaking of some incredibly high level, so that he finally could be free?

"What?"

"Never mind," she said, "tell me, please, when you left your Zen temple, that you said was corrupted, did you throw out everything? The child with the bathwater?"

I almost said no, of course not, please, the child is important, the little child of innocence, of curiosity, of faith in doors that will open if the inquirer knocks politely, the dear little toddler, "the child within" that New Age was propagating until it went out of fashion, but there was something in the woman's pale eyes that made me cautious. Was this another trap to fall into? Was she testing my insight? We had just about reached the East American shore, Land of Puritanism and Positive Thinking. Why shouldn't I throw out the bothersome child with the dirty bathwater? What did I care, anyway? Was I trying to impress this woman, whom I would never see again once we had been through Immigration and Customs? "Yes ma'am, I threw out the child with the bathwater, and the bathtub, too. Out with the Zen child and its filth and its paraphernalia—who needs it?"

"You must have needed it for a while," she said. "But don't yell at me. I have given up on most everything too. Most realistic folks have. There's nothing to hold on to. When you are my age you either know that or you try to become demented. I thought maybe my money mattered, and my art, of course, experiment with colors and forms and shapes when you have the artistic inclination." She shook her head. "I tend to overdo things."

I remembered that Roshi didn't forbid his disciples to pursue artistic interests. There was a student who had a piano set up for him in a neighboring temple; another worked daily hours in a painting studio. "Got to do the little things, too," he said when I said that, if I didn't go mad, suffer a delirium, jump off a cliff maybe, I planned on being a writer. He shrugged. "The ten thousand words." Later when I saw him watch baseball on TV, he laughed. "The ten thousand balls. Some of them make it."

My confessor, the old lady in the Boston-bound airplane, was talking again. "But the little things, even if they seem basic for a healthy routine, for me, don't matter much either. I'm ready to drop them when the time comes. Why carry weights? What do you do now?"

"Nothing," I said peevishly. "I carry along nothing." Then I looked up. I had recognized the koan the old woman had brought up for me again. I told her about it. Once again old Joshu, with his "throw it away":

A monk approaches Joshu. "When I bring not a single thing, what do you say?" Joshu said, "Throw it away." The monk said, "But Master, I have nothing. What can I throw away?" "Then carry it along," Joshu said. Hearing the master say the liberating words the monk became enlightened.

I don't know about enlightenment. When I tried to talk to Roshi about enlightenment, the "satori" I had been reading about in Dr. D. T. Suzuki's Zen guide, on the long ship's journey from Europe via Africa to Japan, Roshi said, "What? Satori? Please? Where did you dig that up? Throw that out." In a way, even then, in my mixed-up embryonic start of the quest, I got that. The last part of the throw-it-out koan exaggerates. It's probably just a bad translation. Can't the monk just get it? The word *enlightenment* comes from Western positive thinking, from putting value on things. Everybody is enlightened. It just doesn't always show. It shows in true love, and after the second double bourbon, and at sunsets, and at death. I knew a smart professor once, who was always looking for the answer. He did a lot of medical research and has procedures named after him, but none of these scientific answers seemed to make him happy. Just before he died he sat up, looked at his girlfriend of thirty years, smiled, and said,

"Of course, how stupid of me, darling, how very stupid," and lay down again and discarded his body. "He knew it all the time," she told me later, "but he was kind of dense."

"What did he know?" I asked.

She poked my side with her elbow. "You know that. That it doesn't matter, don't you think? All this concern of his? All this petty worry? In spite of his brilliance he was very egotistic. It was keeping him back. His death released him."

"From being egotistic?"

She nodded wearily. "Yes."

"Do you carry it along?" I asked my aged airplane companion.

She grinned. "Not right now. Probably when my son meets me in Boston. He lives off me, you know. I consider him to be a burden." She grinned again. "But maybe not this time. What was that koan again?"

Seeing into Your Nature and Other Pastimes

While living at the monastery in Japan I noticed a lot of activity having to do with the spiritual development of the monks, which, in Zen parlance, was called "seeing into their nature." They weren't just sitting quietly in the zendo or working in silence in the gardens, they were talking a lot among each other. Not having any language to speak of (or with) yet, I didn't have much idea of what was going on, but gradually, as I picked up words, I began to catch on. Up till then Japanese had been an exotic language to me. I thought that most everything that was said in Kyoto had a deeper meaning. Kyoto is the spiritual heart of Japan, or, as other local experts told me, a projection of "true Japanese nature." Any day I was out of the sodo I saw senior citizens, brought in by the busload from all over the country, being guided along the neighborhood of temples, halls, palaces, and living museums of religious folklore. The old folks seemed somewhat in a hurry to learn to "see into their nature," before priests back in their hometowns would chant their funeral rites. Dressed in formal kimonos, immaculate black for the men with their shaved skulls and white wispy beards, purple and gray for the women who were often bent double with osteoporosis, the seekers for final insight stopped at every shrine. They bowed and clapped their hands to summon Buddha, the bodhisattvas, Shinto deities, even the spirit of a long-dead emperor when they faced the former Imperial Palace. They all looked serious and devout. The first time I was aware of emotions of a lower level was when Han-san, my English-speaking monk friend, and I overheard a conversation of two giggling old ladies who were bowing to the Temple of the Thousand Buddhas. Han-san pointed discreetly and whispered, "Second Buddha on the third row, the one with the movie mustache—the ladies were saying that he looks like a lover they shared fifty years ago." As I learned Japanese I began to understand overheard conversations, in a streetcar or a bathhouse. None of them had anything to do with "looking into their nature"; it was like home, all gossip, complaints, showing off, exchange of trivial information or, in the case of young males, rough talk. It was a disappointment to know that, in this heavenly temple town, I was definitely not in heaven. However, as the president of a Dutch Buddhist club was to say to me many years later when she heard that a speaker had canceled a lecture she had planned, "I have suffered so much in this life already; this can be added, it won't increase the pain."

I should have known better anyway. I had gotten used to a lack of esoteric meaning in Japanese everyday conversation on the French cargo/passenger vessel that took me from Saigon to Kobe, the last lap on my liberation journey in 1957. Two young Japanese engineers were returning from the Vietnamese jungle, where they had overseen local laborers collecting scrap metal (the war with the French colonial government hadn't been over that long, and the American army hadn't arrived yet). The engineers liked the French apple brandy the *Anna Marie*'s bar was stocked with. They would show each other (and what the hell, me too) photographs they had bought in Saigon of tall nude blonde women and shout *"yosh"* (okay) and *"tai-hen"* (very) as they pointed out the models' dimensions. Didn't I think so? Sure I thought so. They shouted *"Kampai!"* (bottoms up) when they raised freshly filled glasses, but with me their toast was invariably *"Bussho"* (Buddha nature). I never had the impression that they were making fun of me. They had asked me why I was going to Japan and I had told them I was looking to "realize my Buddha nature." They didn't understand me at first, but I copied out the characters for "Buddha nature" from a footnote in a D. T. Suzuki Zen book and showed it to them at the bar. They nodded. Bussho was yosh (okay), too. The pictures of the naked blondes were put away for the moment. They showed me photos of elephants pulling disabled French tanks from under palm trees. "See, that's me sitting on Big Jumbo." They told me that Kobe steel, cooked from the dead French tanks traveling in the holds of the *Anna Marie*, would be shipped to the States where new Vietnam-bound tanks were being built now. They saw much profitable business coming their way. "Kampai!" "Kampai," I said. "Bussho!" "Bussho," I said. They banged on the bar. "Monsieur Steward? Another apple brandy for Looking into His Own Nature here."

I felt like a character in *The Razor's Edge II*. The first version, by Somerset Maugham, had made an impression on me. A young man, heir to a fortune, sets out on a spiritual mission and recognizes, after some meditation and soul-searching exercises prescribed by a guru, his true nature in a hermitage in the Himalayas. A new man, he goes home to Chicago, gives up on his upper-class status, and becomes a cab driver, "to help the other people out," but the book doesn't say how he aims to do that. The hero just wanders off the last page, looking insightful and happy. I wouldn't mind I thought, drinking applejack with Japanese tank recyclers, helping the other people out either, but I'd need to get to know something first—to help out with. My true nature, presumably. It all seemed very tricky, especially when the other people only wanted to look at naked blondes and help build better killing machines. Maybe there weren't any other people in need of being helped out spiritually, which would suit me fine—I would just take off for bliss in the void.

The monks of Daitoku-ji seemed to be getting results in this field of investigation "into their own nature" by solving koans at great speed. Han-san, from time to time, would show me his list of getting there, or getting "nowhere," as, being a true Buddhist, he preferred to call it. The list showed koan titles on the left side, tick-off marks on the right side. He also studied poetry puzzle-books. Roshi, in sanzen, would indicate part of a poem in one book and Han-san would have to find a matching piece in another book. Han-san said he was good at it. Completing a holy poem usually took just a few days of reading and rumination. He said he was gifted in literature. He had noticed that I liked to read too, and got me translations of novels by the Japanese genius Tanizaki. I really liked Tanizaki's writing, the way things twisted into each other, the long monologues, the descriptions of moods, the aberrations of human behavior minutely described, with a comforting but hopeless undertone and always little touches of nature: a bird sings, a cloud passes. But there was no way out; the intelligent reader knows all this will end in terminal madness.

"Of course you like Tanizaki," Han-san said. "The man is totally neurotic." He bowed enthusiastically to express his admiration. "Try Kawabata next. Very sad, and his tales go nowhere too. He and Tanizaki both have the same nature."

I didn't like this. Why would I like neurotic natures?

"Because you are crazy." Han-san laughed. "What are you blundering about here for? What good will all this agonizing do you? Do you have any pleasant goal in sight? I am going to be a priest at a temple in a happy town somewhere, not part of a training ground like this business here. There'll be no sweat in my temple, no stink, no boiled cabbage, no lukewarm bath once every nine days. Flush toilets instead of holes in the floor, home to bird-sized flies waiting for the holy ass. I'll be eating sushi for dinner weekdays, and delicacies the good folks bring in during weekends. There'll be a car! You had all that. You gave it up because you were *curious*, you say?"

"You have no curiosity?" I asked furiously. I pointed at the sky. "The creation doesn't make you wonder? What does it all mean, man?"

Han-san playfully punched my stomach. "Doesn't mean shit, man-san." He punched me harder and made an angry face. "Form is emptiness. The ego is empty on all five levels. There is no suffering because only the ego is suffering; once the ego pops, pain pops with it." Han-san was getting himself all worked up, dancing around me on his clackety-clack geta, punching me every time he got close enough. "You chant the Heart Sutra with us every morning, singing 'Mu this, mu that' in your creaky voice, making us laugh, making the head monk yell at us afterward. Chanting the Heart Sutra, with all the percussion going on, the drum droning, the gong clanging, is supposed to make you look into your true nature by hypnosis." He pointed at his list of solved koans. "They all say the same thing. *There is nothing there.* You still don't get it? That everything is empty? That there's nothing to carry around? That all we have to do is enjoy our nonselves? I'm going to drive an empty car and eat empty sushi once I graduate from here. Maybe meet some empty women while I'm at it. What kind of emptiness are you going to do?"

I hit him too, to make him stop hitting me—maybe too hard, for he ran off.

Some company arrived at the temple, two American graduate students, fluent in Japanese, who wanted to add Zen Buddhism to their collection of credits. They came with impressive recommendations and Roshi had accepted them as temporary students provided they would attend some arduous meditation weeks and see him in sanzen a hundred times or so. Future Ph.D.s at first-class U.S.A. universities, Adam and Trevor told me they would like to solve some koans and get Roshi to give them a certificate at the end of their stay in beautiful Kyoto. They bought motorcycles and rented comfortable quarters in a private house halfway between the sodo and the Willow Quarter. They were friendly fellows. "What koan are you on, Jan?"

I was on Mu.

They had done a lot of homework. They knew about Mu. There was, Adam said, nothing to Mu. The story is obvious. Of course the puppy dog has Buddha nature, the monk knows it, the teacher knows it, and the question is silly. Everything has Buddha nature. The universe is, in essence, divine. The monk is testing the teacher. That's what happens in a lot of koans. Monks challenge masters. Right? Right. Now then, why is the Mu koan so important? Why is it called a gate koan? Why does it offer an opening out of the maze where we, developed human souls (undeveloped souls don't even know there is a maze), are looking for real answers? Because the teacher strikes the monk down with this great shout of "Mu!" The teacher's answer goes infinitely beyond the question of the puppy dog (a lesser creature—the teacher is Chinese, Chinese eat dogs—the dog could be a pig here, or a louse, or the little simple life-form that causes syphilis) being as holy as anything else. Mu means the valueless void, the absolute nonexistence of anything. It is empty space with the idea of "space" taken out; it is zero with the ring removed. Mu takes the Micky out of all monkish questions.

Trevor knew about Mu too. The answer to the koan is "Mu." The monk shouts "Mu!" at the teacher. The void is filled with the void. No more room for questions. Right?

"Tell Roshi," I said.

They told him, seven times a day during the first week of December, which is the toughest week in Zen training and students keep seeing the teacher in between lengthened meditations and very short meals and naps. "I am a cow," Larry told Adam during a break. "I shout 'Mu' so much that's what I am now, a fucking cow, man." He held his hands behind his ears, stuck his face into Adam's face, and bellowed "Muuuuu!"

Adam asked me whether I was making any progress, since I had been there for some time now. What kind of answer was I giving at sanzen? I said I wasn't getting anywhere but that Roshi had told me, in case I was moving without me being aware of it, not to count any passing milestones. Just keep going, and, sure, I was still saying "Mu" too, sometimes. Mostly I said nothing. Roshi would ring his bell again. I would leave, be back a few hours later, say nothing, Roshi would ring his bell again.

"What pisses me off," said Adam, "is these monks making progress. They are only here for their careers, or because their parents threw them out. This Han-san guy showed me his list of solved koans. He says he will be a priest next year. He'll wear a white robe under his gray robe. Different socks. Some kind of colored shawl. He'll be asked to join other priests in another temple for ceremonies, with chanting and dancing; he won't be before the mast anymore, he'll be sailing his own temple. But will he know anything?"

Adam complained that Han-san didn't have the right motivation to solve koans, while he, Adam, had. He was a genuine student of Asiatic advanced thinking; so was Trevor; and even I, although they thought I was there to get therapy for troubles caused by a trauma picked up in World War II, could perhaps be classified as a genuine seeker. So how come Roshi wouldn't let us in on the Mu koan, which we obviously, all three of us, understood? Any practically unlettered farmer's son coming in from the country passed it in a few months or so. Why not us? Didn't Roshi like foreigners, perhaps? Did he believe in Japanese superiority, to the point where he denied the possibility of insight in a gai-jin, an outsider?

Trevor mentioned Roshi saying he had been in Manchuria during the war, as a soldier in the Imperial Army. Roshi had been a monk when the war broke out, but monks had to be soldiers too. If they refused for religious reasons, the Kempetai, the Japanese military police, would arrest, jail, and eventually kill them. Not being a warrior, Roshi had volunteered for guard duty, which was granted because of his poor health. He had meditated while standing still, holding on to his rifle. "The enemy could have come driving tanks at me and I probably wouldn't have noticed." "Interesting," said Trevor, "but what was he guarding? Manchuria was where the heavy war industry was, run by an enslaved population, but there were also facilities where Chinese POWs were used in terminal experiments, there were biological weapon factories, there was all sorts of bad stuff to be guarded there." He wobbled his eyebrows. "You know?"

We stubbed our cigarettes in an empty beer can hidden behind a stone overgrown with moss that marked the grave of a famous Zen saint and went back to the zendo for another three hours of meditation. Well, so what. I preferred to appreciate Roshi on his present level, rather than worrying about his war past. I thought there was karma there, unavoidable circumstances, determining the where and when of a human birth. Roshi's birth as a Japanese around 1900 would irrevocably lead to him being a soldier, a guard—at a mustard-gas factory, perhaps. (He could have been guarding sake bottles—who knows? I certainly never asked him.) Because of different unavoidable karma, Trevor and Adam happened to be born as good Americans, to live splendid lives that nobody would ever be able to find fault with. By chance I was born as the son of an anti-Nazi middle-class Dutch couple, which, according to current values (1940 to 1945, when Germany occupied Holland), made me a good guy too. My karma made me feel good but soon led to doubts, too. What on earth is "good"? Two boys at the school in Rotterdam that I attended were identical twins, blond and blue-eyed. They were fifteen years old; I was nine. I fell in a moat once and they got me out. Once the hated Occupation started, my heroes became German citizens. Their parents had been German but had left Germany before the war for some business reason. Once settled in Holland, they became Dutch nationals. New laws made by the Occupation Authority reversed that choice. The boys were conscripted by the Nazi bureaucracy, and came to school one day in Hitler Youth uniforms on a motorcycle and sidecar, part of the propaganda that was heating up at that time. What fifteen-year-old boys will refuse to show off a motorcycle and sidecar? Their jealous anti-Nazi classmates ganged up on Humpty and Dumpty Heil Hitler, as we had called Heinz and Hans since we discovered they had been relabeled. We regular Dutch boys (I stood back, but I didn't help them either) were going to kill these hateful outsiders by banging bricks on their heads, but a teacher broke up the melee and told the victims to go home and change into civilian clothes, quoting a fictitious school rule that forbade the wearing of uniforms in class. Heinz and Hans went back to Germany later in the war and died in the firebombing of Dresden. Once I heard that, I felt even more sorry I hadn't defended them when the good boys were about to throw bricks because karma had gotten Heinz and Hans a motorcycle. But I still, dutifully, hated all Germans.

"Roshi doesn't hate foreigners," I said. "I heard him deliver a *teisho* on the subject, a Sunday morning lecture in the big dharma hall, with the percussion orchestra going, with all the lay supporters of the temple present, a big gala occasion. The monks were dressed up in their Sunday robes and I wore a tie and a jacket. The monks had been laughing at me, saying that a clumsy foreigner who pisses like a horse cannot realize his true nature. Roshi told them off about that. Everybody has the Buddha nature. He told them that Joshu didn't always say Mu. He sometimes said U. U means everything, everybody, even foreigners who piss like horses."

"You don't speak Japanese too good," Trevor said. "You're sure Roshi said that?"

I told him Roshi had appointed Han-san as an instant translator. Roshi spoke slowly; Han-san whispered the translation into my ears. It was important that I got what Roshi was saying.

Adam also thought that Roshi didn't hate foreigners. He didn't think Roshi would hate anyone. "He can't. I think he is beyond any value system."

Trevor, Adam, and I eventually came up with a theory that suited us better. We were being discriminated against by Roshi, sure, but for excellent reasons. We were superior students, more idealistically motivated than the career-minded monks who only put up with the austerities and stress of their three-year stint in the sodo to become luxurious priests in comfortable temples later. Trevor and Adam, as students of the humanities, specializing in Japanese religion for now, and I, trying to find a cure for an affliction that I insisted on defining as "philosophical curiosity," were serious and intelligent students inquiring into the mystery of the universe. For monks who merely wanted to be priests in nice temples, Roshi, used a kindergarten method of staggered goals that could be easily reached. However, Roshi was guiding *us* in a difficult, but, in the end, definitely more rewarding way, by keeping us on the Mu, the number-one koan, rather than have us fritter away our energy on the little koans and a bunch of cut-up poems. We, future Maitreyas, were climbing Mount Sumeru straight up, with some occasional dangling from cliffs, while the monks followed the endlessly winding far easier path.

That was nice. We were all happy. We all got through the tough meditation week. We would also be getting through our lives. Forty years later I went to a memorial meeting marking Trevor's death. He became a Buddhist, and had a successful university career. The Beatles sang "Yellow Submarine" as we stood in line to burn incense. His photograph, on a red lacquered table, was framed by candles and two bottles of Old Turkey, his favorite beverage, especially in later years. Adam, also a practicing Buddhist now, is teaching, writing, and translating. I read his writing when I need to be reminded of the time when I was concerned with looking into my own nature. I never found my true nature. Sensei, much later, toward the end of the trying years when I was his student, shed some light on the subject by giving me the Master Toso (known in China as Tou-shuai, 1044–1091) three-barrier koan to work on:

> You beat the grass and probe the Principle
> Only to see into your nature.
> Right now, where is your nature?

It seems some koans can only be answered in anger. Having to memorize the many solemn words of this little story and carry them around between drafty buildings during blizzards and rainstorms began to bore me. "Beating the grass," we (Sensei and I, during many sanzen sessions) had established by then, meant "getting rid of ignorance." "Probing the principle" would be "to be enlightened by Buddha's teaching." The matter of "my nature" remained for many months. What could it mean? Did it exist? If it did, what on earth would I do with my "own nature"? Frame it, hang it on the wall? Burn incense to the thing? What is so important about my nature? Finally some truth dawned. Whoever looks for his own nature is lost from the start. I can find something temporary—my personality—but who, including myself, cares about that? Mostly the personality is boring and irritating. As long as it is used as a polite mask, expressing a little loving kindness in daily dealings, as long as it pays bills, does the regular routine in a pleasing manner, the personality will serve until the day the body, another not too important and temporary manifestation, falters and is no more. I'm not my mask. Surely I'm not my body, either. The body is a useful instrument, to be washed and shaved, fed, treated kindly, but we don't have to get ridiculous here. It doesn't really matter that much. Do we care about the body's longevity, the personality's eternity, do we care to have our minds repeating familiar thought patterns? Who is the Who who cares? There is the story about the monk with the troubled mind who goes to the master to quiet the damn thing. "Can you do that, sir?" "Let's see, my friend. Bring me your mind so I can examine it." "I can't find my mind, sir." "There you are, I have quieted it down for you." "The monk's mind is no longer troubled."

But all this is a play on words. Minds are never untroubled. It's the mind's business to be always busy, always troubled about something. If it isn't one damned thing, it's another. The mind is just an instrument, like a computer, to analyze daily troubles, order them, find a solution. Once that is done, take a nap and shut it down for a while. Put it in sleep mode. I'm not my computer, my mind, my body. What's beyond? Nothing. Mu. But Mu is a word used to express the inexpressible. So, pushed to the extreme, I told Sensei to forget the whole thing. And to forget me, too. There is no me. No me-nature, no real-nature, no true-nature, no nothing. I looked around the sanzen room. "I can beat the grass here forever and probe the principle forever and I'll never see my nature. Why should I, anyway? Who cares?"

"Right," he said, "so your nature isn't there. I knew that." His smile was tired. It was 4 A.M. I knew he had been to a party the night before. He stretched and yawned. "Okay. Next move. Let me tell you about it tomorrow, yes? Your next move has to do with death, one of your favorite subjects." He gestured defensively. "Don't look so upset. So you looked for something that wasn't there. It's human nature, you know." He laughed. He wanted me to laugh too. But I couldn't.

BAD COP, GOOD COP

The second barrier as devised by Master Toso made me realize I had learned nothing. Not just nothing about Nothingness, the core of the entire Zen business, but nothing about dealing with Sensei. I had begun to loathe him by then; I would literally snarl when I saw him moping about the hermitage. I wasn't the only disciple thus afflicted. Another student came to see me to ask if he could borrow a gun to kill Sensei with. I was known to have a small collection of rifles and sidearms—not a very Buddhist thing to have, but there it was—hanging from the rafters of my cabin, well oiled, ready to blast away. My explanation to myself was that wanting to have guns was part of the trauma caused by having been through a war. I had seen German troops marching into homes and dragging people out and worried it would happen to my family too. My father didn't have a gun. He was a peaceful man, nervous about force, and would probably have allowed jack-booted boors to kick us into the green van the German military were using in our part of the city—it never brought anybody back. I thought I could defend our house if only I had a gun and knew how to handle the weapon. I was ten or eleven at the time and became obsessed with weapons. I tore pictures of guns out of the family encyclopedia and tacked them to the wall above my bed. After the war I joined the Auxiliary Amsterdam Municipal Police, probably just to be armed and ready. In postwar Holland there are no gun stores; no permits to own guns are granted. When, in America, I saw all kinds of sidearms, shotguns, rifles, even assault rifles being sold over the counter, I bought a small array of deadly weaponry. Any Gestapo agent walking into my house better watch it. But meanwhile I was supposed to be religious too, which caused complications. Like when I found a man *gassho*-ing (bowing with folded hands) outside my cabin, where we were living on some land that I had bought, adjacent to the hermitage property. My wife and daughter were visiting friends and as it was noon-time I was considering lunch. My unexpected visitor introduced himself as a Hinayana Buddhist, said he prided himself on "sticking to the rules" and wanted to come in in order to have a conversation with a "Zen author." It happened that two blue jays had been fighting at my feeder. The bigger bird won, and the littler one's remains, torn-up and bloody, were lying on the moss below. I hadn't gotten to cleaning up the mess yet. I invited Mr. Hinayana to lunch, which turned out to be a bit of a hassle, for he ate only greens and bread, and all I had was meatballs on spaghetti that I was about to heat in the microwave. My guest had been looking at my assault rifle and Magnum revolver, displayed in their holsters that dangled from the post next to the kitchen table. I took him outside to choose a salad from my wife's garden. On the way back he noticed the jay's corpse. "What is that?" "It's a jay, dear." (In Maine it's okay to call male strangers "dear.") "I know it is a jay, but why is it dead?" he asked, gasshoing to the loser's remains.

I had become irritated with my visitor because he kept insisting that I was a mystic. I don't want to be anything at all. He insisted I was a mystic because "You are looking for Buddha." Now why would I be looking for an Indian prince? "In your prayers," he explained. Did he think I went down on my knees every night beseeching Buddha to show himself in a vision? (His insistence probably also annoyed me because some thirty years before, I had been thinking it would be nice to actually see the Buddha, sitting on his cloud like on Tibetan scrolls: free Buddha, well away from the ever-turning wheel of painful reincarnation, kept going by Mara, deity of illusion. "Yes," Mr. Hinayana said, "that's what you do when you are asking for His grace, *looking for Buddha.*"

"Well, I don't, dear."

Now why was the jay dead? I told him that I am interested in birds. Any bird flying about my property has to stop long enough so I can identify him in my bird book. However, birds never sit still, so sometimes I am reluctantly forced to shoot the little buggers so I have time to study their remains to see if they match the pictures in my book.

He gassho-ed in consternation. "You are kidding."

I said I was not.

"You shot that poor creature of God with that machine gun you have inside?"

I told him that's what I had the assault rifle for. I heard his tires spin on the gravel outside. I ate the salads alone. He never came back. He will never know I am a man of peace, that I have never shot any living being yet (except my twenty-year-old cat, but she was dying in agony and I didn't want to increase her discomfort by taking her to the vet). I just happen to be heavily armed. The fellow disciple who came to borrow a gun wanted to kill Sensei because of some scandal that had just been opened up. He felt, as he put it, "terminally disappointed." The indignant student told me he would shoot himself afterward and leave a note for the sheriff to say it was my gun and to return it to me after closing the investigation. I told him to buy his own gun, but he had maxed his credit cards. He referred to our friendship. "Please, brother." I looked into his eyes and shouted "No!" I hid my weapons after that, remembering what my Amsterdam police studies had taught me about "psychotic behavior in isolated religious groups." I warned Sensei. "You're going to be killed by a madman." He told me not to worry, that it was time to continue my Zen study. I had been away for a while and he hadn't given me my new koan, as promised after I, presumably, cracked the question as to where I would look "to see into my nature." Up came the second riddle as posed by Toso:

> Once you realize your own nature, you are free of "birth and death." When your senses are gone, how do you free yourself?

I realized I was the losing blue jay now. This koan had to do with the game being over, as soon enough it would. Anyone over forty knows how fast time slides in the second half, and I was fifty by then. Would I die calmly, in full control, completely detached, smiling, seeing the ultimate joke of things? Who would be this I that I would be when Father Skeleton came along, swishing his scythe? Why not a calm and happy I? It would probably be full of morphine anyway. In my family people die of cancer, mostly. So I lay down peacefully on the floor of the sanzen room, crossed my hands on my chest, smiled, and freed myself of the cancerous body. I might have known there was another trap here. Sensei, on the sanzen throne, was ringing his bell furiously and yelling. "Out! Out!" Again I had no opportunity to prostrate myself as a token of respect to the Buddha directing me. "Out! *Out!*"

Bad cop, good cop. Roshi had definitely been the good cop. It was probably play-acting. Perhaps no good teacher is concerned with the personality of his disciple. The master's intention is to get the self-centered sluggard to finally give up on showing off his masks. Some of the monks told me how fierce the "old man" could be, swishing his short oak stick, actually hurting them when their ignorance, stubbornness, or slowness got in the way of koan study. To me he had always been kindness itself, doing anything he could think of to guide me on my lonely path in a foreign monastery where I was hampered by lack of language, where I got ill because of the poor diet (he arranged for me to have occasional meals in the restaurants of the quarter). He never even mentioned my drinking. I swear Roshi was amused when, coming home late from a party that celebrated the end of a meditation week, I crashed through the head monk's bedroom with my muddy boots on, destroyed his front and back walls of paper glued on latticework by walking through them, stumbled over his body, and kicked the glass he kept his teeth in. I heard that the head monk, the next day, made a serious effort to rid the temple of my presence, but Roshi just laughed. Han-san's comment was to say that Roshi was using me as a grinding stone, to smooth the head monk's spirit. "So you are of use, you see," Han-san pointed out. "It's called being a prop on the stage of negative teaching."

Sensei, on the other hand, was the bad cop. He was good at negative teaching. There was nothing about his daily routine that could make me wish to want to imitate his behavior. He was sneaky and tricky. He called me into his house once as I happened to pass by and sat me down on the floor of his kitchen. He poured me a cup of stale, cold tea and threw me a cookie that had known better days. He looked very serious. "You have been disappointing me. You're an embarrassment with your sleeping in the zendo. What are you going to do about that?"

I suggested I should leave. I was planning to anyway, but I didn't say that. There was still the argument that my karma had taken me to this place and that I should be facing the challenge, rather than run. There was also the argument that the place was a mess and that the few students. I admired had gone long ago. What was I holding on for? Sensei, with all his personal problems, was clearly diseased by egotism, so why was I still acknowledging his superior powers?

Sensei clasped his hands and looked at the ceiling. Leave? Me? His successor? What foolishness was this? Did I have no sense of obligation? Didn't I know I was to take over from him? Run the hermitage? Be the next teacher in his august line of white light going back all the way to the Buddha's insightful disciple, the Indian Daruma, in 450 B.C?

Appalled by the idea of succeeding the one I by now was considering a failed teacher, one of the many who had lost their way, I left my tea and cookie and Sensei's benevolent though critical presence. I didn't know then that he had, in the course of time, played this trick on many of the disciples, suggesting to his pick of the day that he or she was the chosen one, but pointing out that the crown prince, or princess, still had serious flaws, and urging the potential taker-over to work on bettering him- or herself so he/she could, pretty soon now, take over the sanzen throne.

That night Roshi appeared in a dream, looking as neat as I had last seen him, some twenty years ago, in Kyoto. He seemed to be walking, but I saw that his feet were a few inches off the lawn. I got up hurriedly and bowed, but he waved away my respects and asked what was up. "What's down, sir," I said and launched off in a bungled report on Sensei's failings. Roshi didn't seem perturbed. "Little stiff," he said. "Yes, you're right there, a little stiff perhaps." "Stiff?" I was outraged. "Loose, sir. Loose behavior. Sensei is doing away with all the protective rules. Only his cronies get regular sanzen, and the list of the preferred ones changes every month. He is playing power games. We are looking askance at each other. Remember how in Japan each disciple, even the lowest layman, even I, got to patrol with the stick, in the zendo, to beat on the sleepy ones? Wasn't that a good rule? That way we didn't hit real hard, for the one we were hitting would have his turn to hit us soon. Well now, Sensei only has his close pals carry the stick, so they can beat the shit out of us, sir, and we never get a chance to get back at them. I've been tempted to wait for the fuckers outside, with a baseball bat."

Roshi smiled. "As I said. A little stiff. Come with me." He beckoned.

He floated ahead of me. We left first my lawn, then the bit of woods I owned behind the house. We walked down some fields and were heading for the zendo. The zendo wasn't there and instead I saw a huge dark fortress with watch towers, made of granite. Roshi looked over his shoulder. "Buddhist Dogma City—how do you like it?" Before I could tell him the place looked forbidding to me, as ugly as some of the Dutch Reformed churches I had seen in Holland when I was a child, I noticed a gold spot on one of the huge walls of the fortress. As we approached, it turned out the brilliant spot became a kind of tent, a flimsy structure tacked to the wall. It was made out of soiled brocades. Somehow I knew it was Sensei's abode and I told Roshi that. "Let's go inside," he said, but I asked permission to go in first and tidy up. It seemed I was ashamed of Sensei's thought force, which had created the fancy-fair horror. Inside I saw filthy and torn cushions made of cheap yellow plastic under porno pictures torn from magazines, Scotch-taped to the walls. I began to tear them off and intended to arrange the cushions but there were too many pictures and cushions. Roshi stood in the tent's entrance. "A little stiff," he kept saying. As I left the tent a big wind swept down and tore the tent off the wall. It fluttered toward the Atlantic and disappeared. The fortress still stood, as a bastion of silent strength. "Do you think that tent could have polluted Buddhist dogma?" Roshi asked. I kicked the wall and said, "I wish it had, sir. What is this dogma?" "Look," Roshi said. My gentle kick was making the wall crumble. The entire structure was swaying and falling apart. *"Yosh?"* Roshi asked. I thanked him. He told me I was welcome but that he didn't have anything to do with my liberation. It would have happened anyway. I had thought him up to confirm a path I was walking anyway. "But you do go beyond me, don't you, sir?" I thought he would say "But who are you, Jan-san?" but he smiled and wafted away, pleasantly, quietly, not flapping and tearing like Sensei's tent had done.

There was still Sensei and there was still the koan. The koan dealt with death. How to deal with death? I had seen into the nonbeing of my nature, so how would I die, now that I could command all that detachment?

When I faced Sensei again I had, as was usual now in our encounters, become irritable. I was to die now?

This fool will die, Sensei was thinking, that's all the idiot can be sure of. He'll lose himself, all that makes up his he-ness. Someone else will be driving that new truck he has been bragging about once the body he has been washing and shaving and exercising plus the mind he has been teaching tricks are suitably disposed of. He will be as scared as the next man when Death grins at him. But will our clever fellow admit to that? And has he figured out that there was no morphine in Master Toso's time, that opium only came in with the British, that dying was still a painful business?

Pushed by long hours in the zendo and mowing a lopsided field in between during working "recess" on Sensei's unproductive farm, I lost all control when Sensei's stick prodded me again while he made me ask the much-repeated question: "Once you realize your own nature, you are free of 'birth and death.' When your senses are gone, how do you free yourself?"

I dropped sideways out of my squatting position, rolled about on the floor, wailed, hit the floor with my feet and hands, cursed my demon in Dutch.

"Okay," Sensei said, but there was more to the problem. Now for the third barrier as posed by Master Toso. Extinction. How about that? How about giving up my me-ness? *Then* where do you go?

THERE ARE LOTS OF
LITTLE ENDS

If you are free from the cycle of life and death, you will know where to go. But when the four elements are separated, where will you go?

The familiar rigmarole started up again. What were we talking about here? It was the time of the blackfly, and the pernicious insect, multiplied endlessly in the wetlands that surrounded the hermitage, flew into the zendo and took painful bites out of our exposed flesh. Blood trickled and wounds got infected under puffy skin. Don't move, scratch, or mumble, or teacher's crony, soft-shoeing around carrying the *keisaku*, the cedar stick that will bounce off your shoulders, will make you feel the never-abating wrath of the bodhisattva Manjusri, whose image sits on the altar, staring straight ahead, eternally annoyed by the slow progress of meditators in zendos entrusted to his control. The statue was brand-new, made in a Taiwan factory where religious images are sculptured rhythmically on conveyor belts by workers in color-coded hats. It had been painted garishly. In Japan there was always the dust of antiquity, mellow shades, a patina of the ages that covered the imagery, but in many Western temples there is a rough newness. I always liked the lists of rules glued reverently to antique Japanese temple doors, calligraphed meticulously in magical kan-ji. As I could only figure out a few of the characters, their messages seemed enchanting and magic. The signs at the American hermitage were usually tacked to warped boards, written with a ballpoint and conveyed messages like *No more dead cars behind the barn, remove what is there NOW* or *Shit wheelbarrow patrol to all outhouses Tuesday, no volunteers, this means YOU assemble at 4 A.M.* They were invariably signed *Sensei* in a script that sloped irregularly; they reminded me of cattails around his pond, raped by a sudden rainstorm. I didn't like the pond either. He kept quarrelsome geese there that pooped on the walkway outside the sanzen house. First be baffled by riddles, then slither on green slime. During the time I worked on the extinction koan, death was everywhere. A pair of swans, bought with the idea that their stately presence would dignify the pond, were harassed by the geese. One morning we found their white corpses floating on algae soup. An invasion of huge dying flies filled the zendo with a slow deep buzz; the insects liked to die on our upturned bare feet. A bear caught a calf and chewed on it in the bushes behind the sanzen house; the chomping and smacking didn't elevate our moods.

The four elements. I had no idea what Master Toso had in mind there. The four elements have dispersed? No more air, water, fire, earth? A medieval global warming had cooked the planet out of its galaxial pot? Ah, I finally got it. This referred to my own dead body. My body, composed of air, water, fire, and earth, has fallen apart. It has done its job for years, in its incredible complexity, but some micro life-form caused an irreparable imbalance, or a bullet or knife destroyed a vital organ, or there was cancerous cell growth, or perhaps, in a fit of final disgust, I hung it. Whatever happened, it no longer works. In the preceding chapter the Zen student has admitted to getting panicky during last moments, but that is all over now. The act of physical dying is completed. Now what?

"So?" I asked Sensei.

"You tell me!" Sensei shouted, ringing his hand bell, pointing at the door. "Next time. I just sit here, being mysterious, damn you. That's my side of the deal. *You* can talk. Free from birth and death, you know your destination, now that your body is gone, where do you go? Tell me!"

I could talk. Now what would I talk about? The "extinction" conversation with Sensei reminded me of a meeting with a high-ranking Zen priest in Kyoto, some twenty years earlier. Up till then I had only known Saba-san socially, being introduced to his imposing presence (he looked like a nobleman on an antique woodprint) at a cocktail party in the moss garden of a temple run by an American Zen priest. Abbot Saba was an aristocrat, tall, with an aquiline nose and arrogantly raised thick eyebrows. He wrote an art column in a prominent Kyoto paper. I was told he was in charge of one of the most beautiful Buddhist buildings in the city, housing art treasures valued in the many millions of dollars. The day I met him in a cheap restaurant in town, he didn't look at all like his former self. I wouldn't have recognized the crumpled figure in a simple linen robe without the Zen bib or any other ornaments if Saba-san hadn't waved and summoned me over to his table. He was shoveling noodles into his mouth, but most of them fell out again. He looked at me desperately, dropped his chopsticks, gestured at the waitress to give him her pen and notebook, and wrote *Dentist*, in English. I understood, Saba-san had had his teeth fixed. He was full of Novocaine. His lips were numb. Poor fellow. He wrote *What are you doing here?* I was looking for the head office of Nippon Bank, where some money was waiting for me, sent by my Dutch bank, but I didn't know where the bank was, exactly. Having reached the right neighborhood by streetcar, I had realized it was lunchtime and had happened to stray into the same restaurant as the abbot Saba. I took the pad and wrote the characters for *Nippon Bank*. *No,* Saba-san, wrote, *you can talk*. I talked. "Nippon Bank, where is it?"

He got up, tried to suck smoke from his cigarette, then rubbed out the stub furiously, put an arm around my shoulder, propelled me to the restaurant's window, and pointed across the street. I read NIPPON BANK in giant neon letters that flashed insistently. I thanked him. He nodded, then shuffled back to his noodles and pickles.

It wasn't often that I ran into English-speaking—*writing*, in this case—experienced Zen priests with, I might expect, extensive knowledge of Buddhist symbols. As Saba-san seemed friendly enough and evidently willing to be distracted from the discomfort caused by having several back teeth pulled, I sat next to him and ordered noodles too. Expecting that I might have to wait at the bank, I had brought a paperback Buddhist art book. I showed Saba-san a picture that had been bothering me. A scroll showed the monstrous demon Mara, wearing a crown made out of grinning skulls, who holds, with long clawlike fingers and toes, a wheel divided into segments. The outer rim of the wheel is made of bright orange and red flames. Each segment shows an elaborately filled-in miniature. At the axis of the wheel a rooster, a pig, and a snake keep turning the pivot of reincarnation. Some segments show regular people "having their lives"—going about their legal business, farming, shopping, traveling, doing the dishes—but there are also hells where prisoners are being dipped into icy water or roasted on fires or violated by grinning monsters, then there are heavens where much eating, drinking, music and dance, even outright lovemaking go on. There are animal segments where sheep gambol with lions, and where pelicans and fishes do ballets. I showed the wheel to Saba-san, who wrote *Life*. "Samsara?" I asked, a Sanskrit expression that stands for "life" but also for "illusion." He nodded. He wrote *Painful*. I pointed at the joyful scenes and asked why they were caught up in the turning wheel too. Wasn't heaven supposed to be afterward, free of re-incarnation, as free as the Buddha image sitting well away from the turning wheel, smiling on a cloud? Saba-san shook his head. He wrote *Heaven painful too*. He took a plastic bottle from his sleeve, shook out some pain pills, and swallowed them with a mouthful of sake from a chipped jug. Painful? Please. I pointed at the superior beings smoking bubble pipes to the tune of bongos played by a courtesan. What's so painful about carousing? *It stops*, Saba-san wrote. He pointed at the three ego-demons keeping the wheel of birth and death turning, at the self-serving pride of the rooster, the stupid lazy persistence of the greedy pig, the ever-lasting jealousy of the greedy snake. I saw that the wheel's next segment was a hell for gamblers and junkies. I studied a segment showing corporate people spending five hours a day in traffic, single parents watching commercials, family meetings during traditional holidays that end in fistfights and splits. There was a segment where young people celebrate their youth—fast cars, high, moments, cigarettes and sex, drugs, vodka-laced sodas. *Good times temporary too*, Saba-san wrote. He pointed at the free-flying Buddha miles away from the flaming, turning wheel. *Only nirvana forever*. He paid his bill, my bill too, and left, still looking crumpled. At the door he stopped, pointed at the big neon letters of Nippon Bank again, to make sure I at least got that, the location of my upkeep's source, then came back and made me open my paperback book of art again. His long artistic finger pointed out tiny free-flying Buddhas inside the compartments of the Wheel of Life. He tried to say the word "Inside," but his lips were too loose so he had to get the waitress's pad and pen again. *Inside too*, he wrote. "Hai," I said, although I didn't get that at all. A Buddha in a brothel? A Buddha in a Third World police torture chamber? A Buddha in an idling compact, eager to nose itself another few feet toward a city building where a computer screen needs to be stared at for the duration of the working day? In between fast-food lunches and maybe a cigarette outside the building? Saba-san was on his way out again but came back, gesturing furiously. *Inside. Outside.* All the same thing. Emptiness is form, form is emptiness. Escape is possible from any of the wheel's segments; the Buddha is always there, nirvana, pure being, reality underneath the flimsy ego within illusion, samsara. Saba-san came back for the last time and wrote *Free* before pointing at all the Buddhas in my picture, one by one, while spittle drooled from between his loose lips.

Free in hell, free in heaven, free even here, in the soggy-noodle-and-lukewarm-sake restaurant. Don't be taken in by appearances.

Twenty years later, high priest Saba died of emphysema and a malfunctioning liver. A Japanese acquaintance said, "He was killing his body, for years, never stopped, always drinking, always smoking." "But he was enlightened?" I asked. "For sure," Saba's fan said, "free from birth and death, the abbot Saba knew his true essence."

When Saba-san's four elements dispersed, where did he go? Did he have anywhere to go? Knowing all, could he just lie down and discard a dysfunctional body?

My answer to Sensei, which came mostly from being sleepy, was lying down on the floor of the sanzen room, making my eyes flutter for the last time, imitating the death rattle of an old man.

The body is dead, let the bugs, the vultures, the fire consume it. I don't care. I was never there.

"The end?" Sensei asked. "You're all done now?"

I gave him the same answer he gave me when, not long before, I heard that my mother had died. I wandered about my cabin, filling up a suitcase with funeral clothes, getting ready to fly to Holland to pay my respects to a desiccated eighty-nine-year-old body that, for some considerable time, had been moved about by a demented mind, within the safety of a home for the elderly diseased. Even so, it was a shock to know that she wasn't there anymore. I did see her from time to time. We exchanged postcards. Sometimes, when she had a clear moment and remembered she cared, she phoned me. No more caring phone calls. Sensei came in, hugged me, and said, "There are lots of little ends; there are no big ends."

LIBERATING WESTERN THINKING

"East is East," Kipling said, "and West is West, and never the twain shall meet." Even that famous quotation has become gently dated. East keeps meeting West and the dalliance, however hostile at times, gave rise to the birth of the Toyota, Japanese jazz, a movie harmonizing the talents of Lee Marvin and Toshiro Mifune, much better TV sets. My neighbor in Maine thanks Honda's competition for the fact that his five-year-old Ford product does not rattle. ("They used to, you know, them Fords, but no more, no more. Thanks to them Japs. I fought them in the Pacific. Clever fellers, don't you think?") When the Yen shakes, Dollar and Euro jitter. My made-in-China boating hat shows the slogan BEWARE OF IMPORTS. There is a growing exchange of tourists.

Related ideas rise in opposite hemispheres, and e-mail solidifies cooperation. When the Dalai Lama smiles, the seals on my shore bark. *"When the Dalai Lama smiles, the seals on my shore bark."* That's a koan. Whenever something went wrong at his hermitage, Sensei would pause, rub his nose, and say "There is a koan about that, now which one was it?" In this case he would have talked about everything interconnecting. What was it again? He didn't care for improvisations. Exact quotes were the rule. "A polar bear farts, sparrows fall off the roof in Kyoto?"

"Nothingness," Mu, came to me first when I was reading David Hume (1711–1776), a Scottish philosopher. Hume, a successful teacher, was the author of *History of England,* a standard text in eighteenth-century English schools. He also served as a respected government official who, during a period of unrelenting purposeful Christian thinking, published brilliantly construed theories that undercut the reality of the universe. Knowledge of reality, Hume claimed, comes from observation and experience. Your observations and experiences are yours, different, not mine. My perceptions aren't yours; all they are, are, precisely, *my* perceptions. Even if you and I agree on our observations, your observations are still yours and mine still mine, and our joint effort still does not prove an underlying reality to our joint perceptions. It's not that now we are both wrong, it is that we are now both nothing much in either direction. What else am I but your sensual perception of what you call me? And, bewilderingly, vice versa?

We haven't imagined each other, we haven't misperceived each other, we have just made up ideas of each other, which are not real. So what *is* real? Probably, Hume, supposed, most likely—nothing. Perhaps, he concluded, only a void, *the* void, that holds our perceptions is real.

The Church declared Hume's thinking outright heretical, and he could not be a professor at any of the Scottish universities, but his *Essays, Moral and Political* (1741) won international acclaim and got him enough clout to be appointed to high political office. His negations of importance turned out to be beneficial, both to the society he diligently served and to his own being. When, at age sixty-five, he was dying of colon cancer, he cheerfully wrote to his friends, "I now reckon on a speedy dissolution . . . a man my age, by dying, cuts off only a few years of infirmities."

Why did he not find the absence of reality depressing? Perhaps because, denying the reality of his ego, he had few needs. He liked to play backgammon, have his fireplace roaring, nip some mulled wine, and found his studies of nothingness to be "the ruling passion of my life, and the great source of my enjoyments." David Hume's suggestion that everything, including a puppy dog, has no underlying reality but is part of a magnificent void made it easy for me when Roshi, some years later, told me I should learn to "cruise emptiness," like the bodhisattva Avalokitesvara when he was coursing in the deep *prajnaparamita* (perfection of understanding) as related in the Heart Sutra. I told Hume, but he was dead, and Roshi, who was alive then, that the emptiness of their ideas frightened me, that if I were to be nothing in a boundless emptiness I might be lonely. Roshi laughed and touched my head with his short heavy stick while talking to me in a stripped-down kindergarten Japanese he had devised for our communication. "Not empty, Jan-san, void is pretty busy. All other Buddhas live there too. We all have good time now."

True enough, I do have a good time when I try to let go and cruise nowhere. What *is* can be very irritating; what *is not* is soothing. When I was little, an uncle would dress up in a sheet, prance around in the dark of my bedroom, and make odd noises. The spook's presence made me wonder about the justness of being a little kid on a hostile planet. Then the spook would drop the sheet, switch on the light, and be my uncle. The situation had improved, but I was still doubting the justness of being a little kid on a hostile planet where a spook changes into an assholy uncle. Then both of them would leave the room and the nothing that replaced them made me feel a lot better. "What do you want to be?" the patriarch asks his great-great-grandson when the kid is introduced to his august presence. The kid, who will be Hakuin, reformer of the Japanese Zen sect, doesn't like the pressure and comes up with a wise-ass answer: "I want to be nothing, Great Great Daddy-O." But the future famous sage isn't the only one who appreciates ultimate truth. The patriarch smiles. "Aren't you lucky, my dear. You are nothing already."

Although I was approaching the (concept of the) void, I still worried desperately about values, particularly about the value of the goodness of a God who allowed my uncle to be an asshole and who, shortly afterward, wouldn't interfere when soldiers kicked several of my Jewish schoolmates into a cattle car about to leave Rotterdam Central Station, destined for a death factory cleverly constructed by other nefarious creatures He had personally created. Now who to blame? The creator or His product? Do we settle for the Nazis? Or the Allied democratic liberators who were to get rid of my Hitler Youth pals Hans and Heinz in the firestorm that destroyed Dresden? Or myself, who perceived these causes and insisted on labeling them with price tags? God: one thousand guilders plus. Nazis: ninety-nine guilders minus. Me: ten-fifty plus, less fifteen percent for having a cold and developing the sinful art of masturbation. As long as I would be led to believe in values, I was condemned to blaming God, gods, creators, parents, authorities, even roshis and senseis, and, reluctantly, myself, for what I construed as "It ain't right." "Being deluded by my ego," I was, as a Zen monk suggested once, "moving about painfully in the crawling space of my self's basement." But, he told me, *I* was already saved from this deluding and suffering self. How so? Because *I* wasn't there. So where was this *I*? He smiled. "You still don't get it? You never were anywhere. *You* are nowhere."

The monk, a Korean who was given a hard time by Japanese

colleagues but seemed oblivious to insults and put-downs, impressed me with his simple solution. He was being transferred to a more pleasant temple at the time and told me he was lucky. Buddha took note? Was the ever-trying monk being rewarded for his detachment? I asked, trying to trip him up. Never, he said. Luck comes to the lucky. There is no merit. I liked that idea. I already knew that luck does not come to those who keep trying, a saying my spooky uncle liked to come up with when referring to his worldly success that, in everybody's else's opinion, wasn't all that much and seemed to be due to a fickle fate only. I might prefer to believe there were no rewards, no values, but Holland was filled with them, and just by being there I felt I had to carry Dutch values forever.

As luck had it, another great visionary loomed out of the fog of my troubled perception. The phantom posed a question. "Are you one of God's blunders or is God one of yours?" "I'm not sure, sir." "Well, think about it."

Friedrich Nietzsche (1844–1900) had come to tell me about the illusion of values, and suggested I join the ranks of Superman, he who accepts a reality that was never in need of editing, but that, somehow, can be of use. *Thoughts out of Season* (1876) posited that "life neither lacks nor possesses intrinsic value but that it is man who always insists on evaluating life" (an abstraction of the anecdote where a monk insists that a master evaluates a little dog's intrinsic value). Now where does that get us? To where we can figure out the state of the monk's inquiring mind by asking him what he, the monk, thinks the puppy dog is worth. Joshu, however, does not care about the lack of enlightenment in his disciple's being. He sweeps the whole thing away by raising his cane, popping his eyes, bristling his facial hair, and shouting "Void!"

I hadn't met Joshu yet; I was dealing with Nietzsche's lack of values. My initial enthusiasm got dampened when I read about his predictions. Nietzsche seemed, at first, convinced that average men could never put up with amorality. Doing away with laws would lead to a void they wouldn't be able to face. Take away the pillars civilization rests on? Even if, through wars and devastations caused by nationalism based on collective ego, we are forced to doubt sets of morals that couldn't protect us, we'll come up with a similar replacement. If necessary we'll impose reason from some mythical moral upstairs. Man has done so already in Judaism and Christianity, where suffering is okay because it buys immortality to be delivered in a hereafter. Even if holocausts get so terrible that we are tempted to shout "God is dead," we will re-create Him in some other form because we cannot bear to live without an ego structure. The new God will be just as unacceptable in the new systems. Self-appointed value enforcers, whether atheistic in dictatorial communism or monopolistic capitalism, or divine in the intolerant fundamentalism of TV Christian preachers or Muslim extremists, will once again attempt to enslave the masses. Won't the slaves ever object to their masters' luxurious lives? No, because they are told to accept their present fate only "for the duration." The meek will inherit the earth. At some future date, in either the physical or the astral body, blessings will be theirs. Never now, always later. If there is any abuse on the higher level, that of priests, lords, generals, chairmen, gurus, the guys in the yachts off Hawaii, be sure that a horrible hell will be awaiting these apparent winners. Heaven awaits all slaves, who are losers only for now.

In reality the masters are supermen? Nietzsche wanted me to join the ruling class, the A-class in Aldous Huxley's futuristic parody *A Brave New World*, and live off slaves' labor? I almost fell for the Nazi claim that Nietzsche's philosophy excused their selfish behavior. Further study proved that Nietzsche was, indeed, an idealist after all. I could safely bow, and burn incense at his altar. The mild-mannered professor (he filled the philosophy chair at Basel University on his twenty-fifth birthday) neither preaches a callous acceptance of the law of the jungle nor advocates immediate destruction of all existing institutions. No need to dynamite elementary schools or machine-gun tax officials during their tobacco breaks on the steps of a federal building. Yes, Hume's and Nietzsche's nihilism means that all values are baseless. Yes, nothing is knowable. Yes, nothing can be communicated. Yes, life itself is meaningless. But this is no crying matter. This is a laughing matter. Don't worry, life is great, the greater the more petty and selfish value is taken out. Don't waste time on being either moral or immoral. Use Joshu's mu. Pay no attention to values. Just be. And if, while being, we feel urged to do something, give it our best, for no reason. Even if in the end all comes to naught, we can make use of the given moment. Amorality produces thoughtful, nonbothersome sages who grow a little broccoli and tofu, compose the occasional haiku, are taken fishing by the dog. There will be fewer of us on Earth, and small and comfortable populations will respect a splendidly returning wildlife. We won't need to exterminate each other because, pro-choice, we will not multiply our faults by having all that noisy and costly offspring. Tibet will be free and less compulsive about getting their altars just right. Nobody will waste time on nuking the baby whales. We will drive pickup trucks down uncluttered country lanes while listening to the Paris Double Six. We will e-mail love ditties while flying unarmed spaceships. Just a moment now, you say? Aliens without green cards will lurk behind the asteroid cloud? They eat Earthlings for breakfast? Unconcerned about imposing our values (not even our nonvalues), we will invite them to lunch. This simple gimmick worked for Bedouins in the desert. The rule was to invite each other for a meal, rather than start shooting the minute a silhouette loomed up on a sand hill. Bedouin warriors waved from their high-up camel saddles and called, "Have you eaten, stranger?" Who feels like fighting after lamb stew over couscous? And if the bad aliens kill us anyway? More power to them. May they enjoy the universe forever after. We will just take off for a while. Don't tell them now, but we were never there to start with.

Die groessten Ereignisse—das sind nicht unsere lautesten, sondern unsere stillsten Stunden. (The worthwhile performances—they aren't our noisiest but our quietest hours). Friedrich Nietzsche.

TOMORROW NOBODY HAS
HEARD OF BUDDHA

"What is the meaning of Buddha going preaching for forty years?" The monk asked Joshu. "The maple tree in the garden," Joshu answered. "Don't use the environment to show people what's what," the monk said. "I'm not doing that," Joshu said. "So tell me," the monk insisted, "what is the meaning of Buddhism, sir?" Joshu pointed at the tree. "The maple tree in the garden."

I think this was my first koan, after Mu, and the maple tree wouldn't leave me alone for a while. The effort, possibly, wasn't caused by the enigmatic tree, but by my firm belief that I was made to cross a bridge I had crossed before. I felt that Sensei thought I was going too fast for him, or that he was trying to teach me manners. I even gave the correct answer, making as if I were the maple tree, standing up stiffly, holding my arms out like branches, trying to look beautiful like a tree (it was spring—the maple was in flower), and Sensei did nod, but he still wouldn't let me make my next move. "What about the maple tree?" he kept asking.

What I kept trying to tell him (but he always said he didn't want me to tell him anything, he wanted me to show him), was that it had taken me a while to see the beauty of trees, *and I now saw it*. After the war in Holland, which was colorful enough— exciting things, no matter how horrible, kept happening—my formative years were spent in gray boredom. It was the mood of the country. It seemed like the Dutch couldn't get themselves together to rebuild a system that obviously hadn't worked, or that, in a Nietzschean sense, we were unable to replace a failed deity and its outmoded values. While nothing much happened any- where, school was particularly uneventful. The teachers moved about in their sleep. Pupils yawned through their classes. The French teacher, whom I didn't dislike as much as I did his col- leagues—he never punished anyone but just waited for any dis- turbance to die down before carrying on—was not, one rainy afternoon, in his classroom when the dismal herd trooped in. He left a note on the blackboard to say that he had gone home to kill himself. Neatly chalked letters, square and clear, suggested that we should do the same someday. He regretted he hadn't been able to teach us to read French too well. If he had, he would recommend *Une Saison en Enfer* by Arthur Rimbaud, also Sartre's *La Nausée,* which was written in more simple and modern lan- guage. "Earthly life goes nowhere," my French teacher wrote. "Have these brilliant thinkers show you why; then, once you are convinced, be done with it once and for all. If I am wrong I apologize for having attempted to mislead you. Don't pray for my soul. I'm fairly sure I don't have one."

Having become distrustful of adults, I didn't believe the note could be sincere, but when we were marched to his funeral where stodgy-looking relatives noisily blew noses, I became transformed. Here was an adult who actually was trustworthy. I almost applauded when the coffin got lowered into its gaping hole. The end of my positive thinking had finally come about, was even confirmed by the dead authority I was saying good-bye to. Maybe it was time to follow this original thinker's example. Right then Hume and Nietzsche's spirits made their move. Happenstance made the sun break through rain clouds at that very moment. Finches started singing in the rhododendron bushes. I noticed that we were surrounded by maple trees in flower. I had never paid much attention to trees, but from that moment onward I admired their forms, whether bare, sprouting, carrying leaves and flowers, or dead.

I stood in the sanzen room, showing Sensei my appreciation of flowering maple trees. Of course Buddha had spent time making us ready to appreciate nature's beauty, which is just there, whether we watch it or not, apply value to it or not. What is more impressive than a tree? Joshu probably had a good collection of trees in his monastery's gardens. Buddha sat under the magnificent Bodhi Tree when he realized his final insights and later held up a rose when asked about the meaning of life. Then he left, saying nothing. The beauty of life is expressed in any natural artifact. Beauty goes beyond meaning.

Sensei rang his bell. When I refused to leave the room, he bodily threw me out.

At that time I was having a recurring nightmare. I was trying to get in free at the local cinema, managed by a tall blond young man, impeccably dressed, who used discreet makeup. I had come with some of my fellow disciples, who ran past him without stopping at the pay booth. Their illegal entry clearly angered the manager (who sometimes wore the Nazi swastika on an armband but wasn't wearing it that day), but he didn't stop the trespassers. He did put up his hand for me, telling me to get out. "But you know me," I said, and he did—he had seen me there many a time—but his magnetic blue eyes sparked fire. While I kept arguing, he grabbed my shoulder and roughly pushed me out into the street.

"But you know I know about trees," I shouted at Sensei.

"Tell me what's with the tree," he shouted from the open door.

During my next visit I pointed out that nothing was with the tree in particular. Nothing was with any part of the environment in particular. Joshu probably liked trees, and there happened to be one there, so he pointed at it, but he could have pointed at anything that was part of the immediate situation he and the monk happened to be involved with at that moment. The roots of the maple spread throughout the universe, or, in Zen language, stretch horizontally across the ten directions, and vertically reach the ends of the three worlds. (I had found that answer in one of my books.) All of space, all of time—Buddha dealt with any immediate situation within their borders. He came to teach us how. That was the meaning of his coming.

"There wasn't any tree." Sensei was shaking his hand bell while he gave me the next part of the koan. "You are slandering the old man. I tell you, there were no trees in Joshu's garden."

So we continued our sparring, exactly along the lines of regular koan study. We were back at the set answers to be given for the Mu koan, with Joshu challenging the monk within the limits of language. As soon as the monks say yes to anything, the teacher denies its existence; when the monk says no, the teacher affirms existence. The monk can't win and he isn't supposed to win. A good monk is a complete loser. The entire Buddhist discipline is aimed at having the inquirer truly realize that as long as he holds on to anything, whether a positive or a negative, he will suffer. Only extinction of the self culminates in a state of illumination. The Buddha said so. The Buddha was right.

So was Hume, so was Nietzsche. So was Christ. I had been reading the Sermon on the Mount and found it very Buddhist. Christ cried out on the cross. I was crying out on my meditation cushions as the blackflies tore at my flesh and my bones were hurting.

Toward the end of my connection with the hermitage, I kept a dictionary of Chinese Buddhist terms in my truck. Sensei wanted a lift somewhere and got upset with me for having allowed the book to drop on the floor. It actually showed a footprint on its torn dustcover. He accused me of religious sloppiness. I remembered the lessons the Japanese monks had taught me. Always say "Hai hai" to the teacher or anybody in command, then do whatever you like. If you get any shit, bow and smile. Don't confront anyone. Don't waste time and energy on anger; save your strength so you can smoke Shinsei cigarettes behind the ornamental bushes with other smart disciples. They showed me their hero, Hi-san, the fat cook. As a senior monk with the rank of priest, he had his own room where he liked to sit through his off-time in full lotus, listening to a radio hidden in his sleeve and connected to his ear by a flesh-colored miniphone. He was good at stacking cigarette stubs in small ashtrays. I never saw him in the zendo. I never saw him upset. Whenever the head monk yelled at him, Hi-san would fold his chubby hands, bow, and look sorry before going back to his talk show and cigarette-stub pyramids in his room at the far end of the sodo. "Hai hai." "I am here, listening to you. Yessir, I am here. Being sorry."

"Hai," I said to Sensei. "I am here and I am sorry I dropped my book of Chinese Buddhist expressions, together with the characters expressing them, on the floor of my pickup truck. How inconsiderate of me."

"Apologize to Buddha," Sensei said.

"Tomorrow nobody has heard of Buddha."

He looked angry. "What was that?"

I told him it was a koan I had made up, to replace the "Buddha is a shitstick" koan. A shitstick is still something, but in my koan the Buddha would be totally forgotten. He would meet with a "little end." There are no big ends—there are lots of little ends, but little ends, in their little ways, can be very final. One day for sure there wouldn't be a Buddha to remember that he had been a Buddha. There wouldn't be a universe to remember the non-existence of the Buddha in. There would be no more Zen, ch'an, dhyana, or whatever those totally forgotten masters of the past would care to call their sect, school, path, direction. No space, no time, no Heart Sutra, no path, no no-path. There would only be nameless hanyaparamita.

Sensei wasn't listening.

"Hello?" I asked. "Tomorrow nobody has heard of Buddha."

He made me stop the car, said he preferred to walk to being driven by a heretic, an embarrassment, an ex-disciple. I saw him shake his fist in my rearview mirror as I drove off. I wondered what he would be like the next day. The next day came, with a message delivered by a student. He had written down the message, in case he might misconstrue Sensei's mysterious words. He pronounced them slowly and clearly. "Sensei severs his connection with you, for what is, for what was, for what will be, as you know." He looked at me over his glasses. "*As you know*, you know?"

I didn't know.

"Any comments?"

Zen folks always have great comments; they laugh, they

dance, they become instantaneously enlightened as they understand, fully, without the slightest doubt, the hidden meaning of
their teacher's cryptic message.

I couldn't think of any comments.

"That's it?" the student asked.

That was it then, I supposed. Yes. Probably. That could be
it, then.

Gurus Waft In and Out— Only the Not-Guru Is Real

There is the story of the man who, every morning before breakfast, takes his dog to his front yard, picks it up by the tail, and swings it around a few times. A neighbor who asks why the man treats his dog that cruelly is told, "You have no idea how happy the dog is when I put him down." Having been let go by Sensei, I felt much relieved. It's nice when a guru lets go, but the respite, at best, is temporary. Baba, the airport teacher, had told me that in Hinduism there are all kinds of gurus, and they are all temporary guides, except one, the *sadguru*. The sadguru, who represents our pure being—that which can't be defined—really has us by the tail. (In Zen sayings we find the same idea in "the man without rank.") The sadguru is the inner guru. The outside gurus can be understood as temporary projections of the inner guru. They come and go. They show part of the way. They're hired and fired, and it's the sadguru that does the hiring and firing. Not the personality, not the mind, not the body, nor any entity on any of the ego levels, has anything to do with that painful process, they just happen to be its subject. The *not* guru is the real mover and shaker. Roshis, senseis, and babas serve the sadguru diligently, until he gets bored and flicks his fingers. "You there, out with you. You over there, in with you. Teach our fine friend here to turn some new tricks. Attaboy. You can do it." Baba was very disrespectful when he talked about gurus. "Any teacher is temporary. You deal with them all the time, you know. And there's no reason for them to feel that mighty. The guy who teaches you how to stick your plastic into a gas pump for the first time is a guru too. Or the Samaritan who helps you put together the office chair that came in the mail with instructions in Finnish-English— thank him; he is a valuable teacher. Use gurus, but don't hang on to them. How many times do you want to learn the same trick? Leave when the lesson is taught. If you're too damn grateful they'll make a personal zombie out of you. Don't transfer your power to any outside guru."

As Sensei would say, "There is a koan about that." The subject of what really moves human lives came up one day after dinner and Sensei said, "Remember, it isn't you who controls you," and went to his room to search his files but couldn't come up with the required Zen text. I went home and, thinking I might be of help, looked through my library and copied a seemingly suitable text. Some weeks later, at another dinner, at my house this time, I showed Sensei what I thought was the relevant riddle. He didn't have his glasses with him and waved my paper away. I insisted. "You were thinking of the servant koan, coined by Gozo? Also known as Tosan? Who referred to two Buddhas by name and said that even they, supreme beings, were but servants of someone the student has to identify?" Sensei got annoyed. "Gozo *who*? That said *what* about *what*? Have you been *reading* again?" There were other dinner guests. Sensei pointed an accusing finger, called me "our clever fellow." He told the students that we should stay away from books, that I was a bad example. He stomped out of the house without finishing his dessert, followed by his stern-looking students. My wife was in tears.

At another occasion, when I was on duty at Sensei hermitage for the day, he told me to clean out the sanzen room. I found several Zen books lying next to his cushions. One of them was open, showing the Gozo koan I had found in my library. Sensei, when he saw me looking at his book, told me that he planned to retire soon and was looking forward to "reading for ten years." Later again, we went to some function by chartered bus and everybody, including Sensei, was reading copies of the novel *Shogun* (which the supermarket had on sale) as the evergreens lining the interstate zipped by. I saw a moose and her calf and shouted for attention but they all kept their noses pointed at the neatly dramatized version of a romantic ancient Japan discovered by a Western hero. "This is it, man," a fellow student said. "Makes me wish I can get to Japan someday."

Master Gozo said, "Even Sakyamuni and Maitreya are his servants. Tell me who I am referring to."

I met this mysterious master of Buddhas (Sakyamuni, formerly Prince Gautama of India, being the last Buddha, the future westerner Maitreya being next) in another koan, too. In that riddle Rinzai, a Chinese Zen master preceding the great Gozo, tells his monks, "in your physical bodies, right inside your flesh, there is the unrankable being who often goes in and out of the doors of your faces. Who is he? Tell me right now."

The sadguru does not look for the way, for he is the way (see *I Am That, Talks with Sri Nisargadatta Maharaj*, Acorn Press, 1996). In *The Tibetan Book of the Dead*, an ancient guideline (still in print) for the recently departed, the sadguru appears as the speaker and addresses the ego as "the highborn one." The sadguru dares the personality to step into its white light of eternal enlightenment, to avoid the colored lights that lure the soul into some kind of physical existence.

The ego hasn't had enough yet? It chooses to be reborn again? Very well, the sadguru will, once again, manipulate its karma to teach painful lessons. Suffering will be caused for one purpose only: to remove the obstructing darkness of a false identity. The sadguru wishes to rip off all our masks. The sadguru is the power that drives the stumbling monk, through trap after trap, to Buddha Land, in the Chinese novel *Monkey*, or drags his Christian equivalent, the spiritual seeker in the medieval novel *Everyman*, through Eastern European badlands on his search for God. The sadguru (I am still quoting Airport Baba) may forget about us for a while, but when he remembers us he knows no pity. He'll do anything to get us back to the source of our own pure light. His compassion may appear cruel. He'll make a heroin addict out of the clean-living banker if he thinks that the quest will go quicker that way, or a banker out of the cleaned-up heroin addict if that suits the search of the moment better. He'll buy his student a five-million-dollar yacht, have him sail it on calm seas to a Pacific island where hula girls sway to the rhythm of banjos, then have the boat pirated. Bandits chain the ego to a rock and cut off his pinky, mail it to relatives to urge them to pay ransom. Why? So he can realize his inner nature. Which is what? The sadguru himself. This is a movie? What else is life but an unedited movie? The plot line may seem to go somewhere but soon turns bizarre. Who can make head or tail of his or her own life? Can we ever react adequately to the changing scenario? Do we ever find justice anywhere? How about the senseless repetitions? Why are we always late with our newfound insights? Why are circumstances beyond our control always driving us crazy? When things are right for a change, how come we can't hold on to them? Why isn't there ever time to get used to anything, not even to discomfort? The plot moves on. Like the White Rabbit, always late in *Alice in Wonderland*, the ego rushes on blindly. Into death. Into birth.

But is it *me*, living through all these sometimes pleasant, sometimes painful movie sets? Please tell me it is me, I wanted to beg Baba. Let something be consistent. "Not really, you know," Baba told me during our long snowbound togetherness at Logan Airport. Personalities last for one lifetime only. New birth, new me. Me One would never recognize Me Two, but then, it doesn't have to. One and Two don't, except perhaps in brief déjà-vus, share the same times and places.

How sad? He advised not to worry too much about the apparently senseless ups and downs of my many lives, for no part of the rigmarole matters. It's all showtime. Some make-believe lives are quick, some seem a little slower. Up pops a life where we are positively brilliant, next comes a murky passage where we are retarded. Now we come nice, now we come nasty. The hunchback and the beauty queen. The one gets repaired, the other grows old. We yo-yo, but the ups get higher, until, eventually, each of us, Baba promised, after six hundred lives or so, reaches the top of Mount Sumeru. The pinnacle will be under our feet, in spite of all our resistance, for the ego never cooperates—it wants a comfortable niche and it wants to stay there—but the sadguru won't have that. The true self brings on war and pestilence, just to force the ego forward. If nothing else works, the unavoidable prospect of death will make the slowest of students pay attention. "I'm busy," the doctor tells the bogus personality, "but I'll take the time to explain your position. Your liver is shot and I'm not going to fix it. I could try if you had more insurance, but even so, the case would be ninety-nine percent hopeless. Go home, have a good cry, write your will, and wait for Old Bogey." What if even death doesn't wake us up? Well, there the hero wanders about in the bardos, purgatory, the afterlife, mistakes his next mother's entrance for a nicely lit-up gate to some exotic pleasure quarter, doesn't think, slips in, gets pulled out again nine months later, comes to his senses, and, once again, phrases the same question he has had hundreds of times before: What did I get myself into?

The prospect didn't cheer my personality at all. It looked around Logan Airport, where thousands of other stranded personalities hung about sadly.

"Ha," Baba said. "You think you are alone? Aren't I here too? Just one life ago I was a lord in a palace. The concubines overfed me. I died of a bad bleeding. Wandering about in the bardos I didn't pay attention and, *whoops*, got reborn in a cardboard box in Calcutta. Grew up to be a starving Brahmin, turned pariah cleaning tables, and now I am Mr. Holy frightening you with true tales. Ups are good. Downs are good too." He tweaked my cheek. "I tell you, just keep going."

"To where, Baba-Shrih?"

A Zen master would have slapped my face and shouted at me to answer my own question *right now* so that I would become instantly enlightened to fit some future koan. Baba took the time to explain his answer patiently. My search was destined to turn out just fine. All human beings get done at about the same speed. In most lives there aren't, not really, too many shortcuts. Make some progress in one life, learn more by falling back in the next one. Human beings get reborn some six hundred times, give or take a few lives, before they drop their nonsense, acknowledge the whole thing was a game, thank or forgive the other players, laugh, and move on to a higher order of being. Remember your Buddha's sayings? Baba asked me. When Sakyamuni was asked what life was like at the end? Didn't "He Who Knows" say "I am always at the beginning"?

999 Ways of No-Direction

You call things up and they won't leave you alone. Why provoke a Far Eastern genie? Born in the West, I never meant to get "into Buddhism." Hume and Nietzsche having passed on, I just wanted my nihilistic theories confirmed by living masters. In 1956, after I finished reading a prescribed list that started with Plato and ended with himself, Alfred Ayer, a British philosophy professor (*The Problem of Knowledge*), suggested I should read Meister Eckehart. Eckehart, a Dominican monk, "father of German mysticism," 1260–1327, was a master of negation, so much so that Catholicism would no longer accept him. I studied the material and told Professor Ayer I would like to be Eckehart's disciple. The professor followed up on my joke. He told me living masters of the meaningless way could only be found in the Far East now. He recommended Japan. Tibet might be better, but it was about to be taken over by China, and it was cold there and I would have trouble learning the language. ("And their ceremonies are endless, you know—you're sure to get bored.") China was communist and had begun to persecute its own Buddhist and Taoist masters. India could be good (he told me Hinduism would suit my purpose fine too), but he had heard that dysentery was rampant and medical service poor. Besides, there was all that poverty, which tends to lead the happy thinker astray. No, Japan was just the ticket. "A hygienic country, owned and run by intelligent and clean-living people, on the up-and-up now. Yes, you will like it there, my boy."

I did like it there, but there were some drawbacks. On leaving Kyoto, I thought I was done with chanting sutras and getting up at 3 A.M., with painful meditation and blundering along in a very foreign language. I didn't think I had learned anything from the intelligent and clean-living people. My ego was too dense, my personality too vain, my mind too restless. Watching Japan's coast fade in fog, I turned toward the ship's bar, planning to drown my soul in cold beer.

The sadguru, if such a power exists, let me do that for a while. Then the whole business started up again.

In Holland, in the early sixties, a TV producer called to ask if I was a Buddhist and if I wanted to be on TV. Imagine. There are the relatives and the friends and the colleagues and the customers and the fellow reserve policemen of Amsterdam, watching episode number fifty-seven of their cultural Thursday evening program and who shows up? My very own ego.

As for the first question, no, I wasn't, precisely, a Buddhist.

But hadn't I studied Buddhism in Japan? The producer had heard that somewhere.

I began to describe the Hume-Nietzsche-Eckehart connection.

"That's okay," the producer said. "You can explain all that on-screen."

"What is this about, sir?"

About, the friendly voice explained, whether life has a purpose and if so, what? This was the title of his show's next episode. I was to be on a panel, with a theology professor, a bishop, a Dutch Reformed Church preacher, a humanist. He had planned me as "relief."

He was looking for a comedian?

Well, maybe yes, the friendly voice said. Christians tend to be heavy and humanists wordy and theology professors even split syllables and commas, but he heard that Zen Buddhists (it was Zen that I had studied? Good, good . . .) like to give short, kind of humorous but to-the-point answers to weighty questions. Could I do that?

On TV? For sure.

He wasn't too far away and would I care to share lunch? He wanted to check me out, okay? The show was taped and awkward scenes could be cut, but why waste money?

At lunch, he was pleased to see that I was neatly dressed and had short hair. I signed a contract. It would be all right to tell my wife and friends about this. Could I do him a favor? Promise there would be no four-letter words or lewdness? He didn't think I was that type, but just to make sure?

The humanist (a lady who told me God is possibly dead but that's no reason not to be loving) and I sat at one end of a long table. Christianity took up the rest of the studio's space. We all had microphones and strips of hard plastic that gave our names and a brief description of our qualifications. Mine said ZEN BUDDHIST. The bishop was obese, short of breath, and had a deep, rumbling voice. The professor, so tall and dry-looking that it seemed he would break in two whenever he raised his hand in protest, kept reminding the audience, before answering questions, that he held appointments at two universities, not, please, just one. The preacher looked nondescript but angry. First we had to state whether we believed in a purpose. Professor and priest said, Yes, God's purpose. The humanist said, Yes, Our purpose. The bishop said the question was irrelevant and I said I didn't know. The producer asked the theologian and the preacher who, exactly, was God. And how did God wish us to serve Him? Did we have to take the Bible on faith? The theologian and the Dutch Reformed preacher produced many arguments that proved the supreme being's existence, which were, as eloquently, defeated by the humanist lady. The bishop said that now that he was old, sick, and in doubt of his achievements, he sometimes felt close to Him, that he felt fear of getting closer and that if he ever were to see God face to face he certainly wouldn't discuss the idea of "purpose." Now then, the producer asked the humanist, if we were to qualify our purpose, as she kept saying, as a self-appointed obligation to serve fellow humans, where did that take us? In a polluted city-state of sixteen million gridlocked people like Holland, that was getting more overpopulated by the day? How about diminishing some future numbers? Was she aware that, worldwide, humanity was multiplying itself while being terminally cramped for space? What were her thoughts on a program of obligatory snipping and tying of sperm- and egg-producing tubes? Wouldn't humanity be best served by getting rid of, say, sixty percent of a future generation? The humanist, hurt by the producer's iron-fisted hammering, lost her composure. "Just be nice," she said, blowing her nose. "Just be nice. It'll work out. Mutual love will save us. Please."

I just sat there behind my two strips of plastic, one long one with my name, one short one with my label, waiting for another half hour of yes-or-no-purpose-life to pass. It didn't look like the Zen Buddhist view was wanted. My turn came, however, for the raging battle between the theologian and the preacher (how could

God be questioned?) became rowdy, and the producer shut them up. He addressed me. He passed me a note that called for a "light yet tragic" end. He verbally conjured up a suitable scene: Imagine an old woman dying alone in a hospital room. I am visiting someone but I have lost my way and I find myself next to her bed. She is reaching out to me. What do I do?

I tried to visualize the unfamiliar setting. "Is there a chair?" There was? I said I would sit down. I would hold the lady's hand. She is reaching out, isn't she? She is putting out her hand? Very well, I would hold it.

Silence crept into the screen. Silence is not good on TV. TV is always busy. The old woman is unbusily dying. We want some action here. "Terminal case," the producer said sadly. He was giving me other clues. Autumn leaves were falling, the old woman and I saw that, through a window. The producer said it again. "Lea-ves fal-ling." I knew what he was hinting at and I was aware of my wife, child, relatives, friends, and their pets watching me sitting there with all these respectable, well-meaning people, but I wasn't going to tell a dying woman that there had been a purpose in her life because the leaves were falling outside and would, next spring, grow again, and that everything renews itself and that she should become a Buddhist so she could believe in reincarnation and not feel so wasted. The old woman *was* wasted. She was also alone. She was probably in pain. She was frightened, for she was reaching out to me, a stranger. She needed someone to hold her hand and I was doing that. Please let us share a quiet moment, the old woman and I.

The producer got desperate. He was pointing at the clock, which was out of view of the camera. His clasped and unclasped right hand, symbolizing a talking mouth. The professor and the preacher were miming messages too. Save that woman! Get some God into that terminal hospital room. The bishop had trouble breathing. He pointed a heavily ringed thick finger at the ceiling.

Did he want me to call an angel? The humanist lady was smiling her encouragement. Be nice be nice! Hug that poor woman. Make sure she, an old woman without relatives, neighbors, or friends, hasn't spent a useless life. She always fed her goldfish. She cared. She must have. She is human, isn't she now? Tell her how much *you* care. How much *all of us* care. The producer kept his voice friendly, for his voice was part of the show. "But what would you *tell* the dying old woman? About the purpose of her life? Was there any? And if so, what? What would you *say*, Mr. Zen Buddhist?"

I was getting desperate too. "Nothing," I said, "I would just sit there, hold her hand, wait for her to die. We would wait together."

"For what? For her death?"

Seemed like a good idea to me.

"Is that what Zen Buddhists do? Help us wait for death?"

This was getting annoying, but my mother was watching so I kept my voice friendly too. "I don't know. I'm not really a Zen Buddhist."

"So what are you?"

I kept smiling, hoping the smile was Buddha-like. Now was my chance to show detachment. If you can't make it, fake it. My wife was watching; she wouldn't want me to hit the producer, and I had promised not to use bad language. My five-year-old daughter was watching too. "Hi, Daddy." My cat, a short-tempered Siamese, would approve of violence, but a man has to make a living. I couldn't abuse a fellow citizen on public television. I was running a business during working hours and being a reserve cop on the side. There are always these considerations. "I'm not sure what I am," I told the producer. "Hopefully, I am not."

Not. What does that mean? The producer sighed.

End of show. Credits.

At the time I was supposedly dealing with the death of a lonely old woman I was beginning to believe that my own effort was not leading me out of the wheel of karma either. The Japanese adventure, no matter how exotic, hadn't produced insights, and my present life of daytime merchant and nighttime cop didn't contribute to the enlightenment process either. I was beginning to think that I should face facts, give up on the quest, be a happy burgher in a country of milk and veal croquettes, when the TV show pushed me in an unexpected direction.

Sources familiar with such matters indicated, the producer told me in a note that accompanied a hundred-guilder check, that one-tenth of all of intellectual and spiritual Holland had watched his show. He forwarded letters from a dozen Dutch Buddhists who wanted to make contact. I invited the members of this sangha, the Buddhist brotherhood, to a meal in a Chinese restaurant. Nine wanted to develop their spirits along formal and definitely moral lines. Three were sympathetic to my nihilistic quest. The four of us set up a common meditation room, a heavy post-and-beam construction, a solid Dutch version of a zendo, on the seventh story of a fourteenth-century gabled house in Amsterdam's inner city. During zazen I was the *jikki-jitsu*, the feared disciplinarian who rings his bell every twenty-five minutes and hits whoever dares to move in between. I only hit gently, like the morning's sunrise, and passed the stick to the next guy during the next session. Dutchmen are allergic to being whacked with a five-foot cedar stick. They tend to wrench the weapon from Manjusri's hands and get back at the meddling bodhisattva. So far so good; nothing basically new happened until the producer phoned again. This time he wanted me to help check out a Tibetan *trappa*, a fully ordained monk, who was allegedly being exploited by two

Dutch ladies. He thought there might be a TV story there and as I was an expert, a Buddhist . . . "I thought we had been through that," I said. He said it didn't matter. Here was a Buddhist in distress. Hadn't Buddhists helped me out in Japan? Didn't one trade invite another?

He wangled an invitation from the ladies, who had the trappa perform Sunday rites at their country mansion. They told us they had found their handsome young man working in a road gang in northern India when they were there to visit holy sites. Dazi-Kawa, liberated from his backbreaking labor by these blue-haired foreign devil women, followed his saviors to Holland. Dutch Immigration issued a visa against a deposit that would pay, in case of trouble, for his deportation back to India. The ladies paid in crisp new banknotes. The trappa saw them do that.

The trappa was a short, slender man with a shy smile who, when the oldest woman clapped, stepped from behind a screen. The other woman clapped too and the trappa chanted Sanskrit texts while hitting a cymbal and shaking a rattle. He was dressed in proper Tibetan robes, purple and yellow. His feet were bare. He stood while he chanted, then sat down, tucked in his legs, said "Hello," in English, and "Happy to be here." After that he cried. The old ladies ushered him out of the room, came back and apologized, said "He keeps doing that—we don't know what's the matter with him," poured tea and offered biscuits with Gouda cheese. I asked if I could see the trappa in private and when they said I could not, I said I would anyway and looked all over until I found him in the attic. Dazi-Kawa told me, but it took a while to understand him as he was still crying and had an exotic accent and few Western words, that he was a prisoner, forced to do vacuum-cleaning and impossible stacks of dishes, that his pocket money wasn't enough to buy anything he needed, and that he couldn't leave because the police would catch him and chain him into an airplane. The old ladies had said so. They were both demons. They had bought him for a pile of cash. "Please help." He folded his hands. "Help wanted."

The producer convinced the ladies that their protégé should be allowed to stay at my apartment in Amsterdam for a week so we could figure out what he wanted. The ladies knew the producer from their screen. They didn't want to be denounced on the culture channel.

Dazi-Kawa mainly wanted to be away from the old ladies and didn't want to repair more Indian roads. I paid Immigration a fresh deposit and the ladies got their old deposit back. The official told Dazi that he was now under my custody. "His slave, yes?" Dazi asked. "His slave, no," the official said. "This is Holland, free country, you just do as Master says, yes? No make trouble?"

We had our troubles, beginning on the occasion when I bought my guest a raw herring at a street stall and showed him how the delicacy is traditionally eaten by holding it by the tail, bending one's head backward, and slipping it into the mouth while chewing and swallowing simultaneously. As Tibetans never eat fish, he wasn't immediately aware that the slippery object was a herring caught in the North Sea that very morning. He told me later, "Maybe bird with slimy tail." When he finally understood what the food had been, he threw up all over his robes, cursed me, and got yelled at by the herring seller.

Later that day, Dazi was fascinated by prostitutes who display their bodies in the washed windows of Amsterdam's Red Light District. As we had taken him to a summer beach where attractive women sunbathed topless, "to improve their skin," as my wife explained, Dazi thought the prostitutes did that too: bathe their nudity in red neon light for its health. As a monk raised from boyhood in Lhasa's immense Potala temple, he only knew the female form from statues where bodhisattvas, male and female, mix yin and yang in spiritual/bodily contact. The idea that prostitutes do it for money seemed new. "You can go see them in their rooms, but you might get sick," I said. He wasn't worried about disease. I could never get him to understand the phenomenon of microscopic low life, even when I borrowed a microscope and showed how a drop of clear water is populated by possibly aggressive beings. Dazi thought microbes were amusing. Having to pay money was a better determent. In his colorful robes he was too visible in the district but he often went there in civilian clothes, to stare, he said, and be amazed. He left no money in the inviting alleys. Dazi desperately saved all his cash. He wanted to "buy himself free" by paying me off. I told him there was no need; I would get the deposit back as soon as he would cross the channel, as he said he wanted to—Dutch was too much for him and he was learning English. He kept saving, however, now to take care of himself if life took a nasty turn again. Chinese soldiers throwing his and his mates' belongings out of a Potala window and machine-gunning anybody who tried to interfere had destroyed his faith in a kindly world. "Next time I am Charlie, take savings and run one hundred kilometers an hour." Charlie was Dazi's second personality, which took over as soon as he changed into jeans, an embroidered shirt, an elegant silk jacket that he had designed and sewn with my wife, and thick-soled sneakers. I had gotten him a room behind the inner-city zendo, and work in the dispatch room of a mail-order business that paid regular wages. The cash could have taken ample care of his few needs, but he preferred getting invited to meals and being given necessities by local Buddhists, Chinese, Korean, and Japanese, who liked him to come over to perform rites. When he left, after two years, to become spiritual counselor to a British entertainment star, his overcoat rustled with a secret lining of hundred-guilder notes. Two enormous suitcases and three duffel bags stuffed with belongings were wheeled on board by a porter I had tipped beforehand. I told him he was a heavy man these days. "I essentially am weightless monk," Dazi-Kawa said as he got on the British ferry.

"You are essentially overloaded layman. You walk heavy way."
He smiled. "Never mind, you too will get there."

"I am supposed to be there already," I said, but he never liked
Zen talk. He didn't like meditation, either. He claimed he had
done enough for several lifetimes, just now, in Tibet. In the Potala, which he had entered as a small boy, he had been forced to
follow the harsh meditative and work training that makes an acolyte into a trappa. "Police monks beat me. Everybody bigger
than me beat me. I bow to everybody bigger than me. Then I
finally finally become ranking monk—trappa, yes? Now little
guys bow to me, carry my stuff, I beat them a little. I have room,
bed, chair, radio with battery, room service, plenty of tea and
butter and nice food. Eat *momos* [dumplings] twice a week. On
white rice. Then Chinese big guys come with rat-tat-tat guns.
Start beating *me* again."

He would sit with us in the zendo, however, and perform
meticulous rituals at the altar. I had decorated the altar with a
collage of toy dinosaur skeletons, Dutch seashells, and a photograph of an oriental nude woman framed in antique heavy silver,
found at the flea market at Waterloo Square. Dazi-Kawa accepted
my explanations. The dinosaur was to remind us of former life-
forms that became extinct, like we would be extinct one day. He
liked that. "Yes, in future some strange fellow has plastic human
skeleton between incense burner and candle?

"And the sunbathing woman in silver window?" he asked.

I said I liked women better than men and that Buddha's physical form, even stylized as an art form, couldn't make me bundle
my mind force. As nude women often entered my thoughts while
meditating, I might as well go for them rather than go around
them.

"And the Dutch seashells?"

I said they also represented the female aspect and were part
of my paying respect to the country I was born into this time.

"But you always complain of climate and your country," Dazi said. "Rain, drizzle, and fog? Low-lying morass? Muddy, wet wastelands?"

Well. Sure. But the country had still raised me. Fed me cheese and potatoes and lots of overboiled greens. Loving kindness at home. Some schooling.

Dazi-Kawa wasn't listening. His arm swept over the altar's attributes. "You mind if I throw out?"

I did mind, but I wasn't going to say so. He did keep the incense burner and the candlesticks. An ever-fresh display of apples and oranges displaced the shells. A fat little Buddha statue replaced what I thought was an image of the delectable Hindu goddess Kali. The dinosaur was replaced by Nothing.

The fully ordained monk Dazi-Kawa was too remote to ever be a friend, but he kept me on the straight and narrow. If I missed early morning meditations he would be bellowing on the phone, raising me from my comfortable bed at the edge of Amsterdam. ("Put ass in Citroën, drive to Inner City, me waiting, tea and ginger snaps ready. Hop hop now. Okay?") He was interested in my struggle with Mu and kept prodding that I should jump into the abyss. "What abyss, Dazi?"

He knew that one. "The abyss where the ego doesn't dare to go."

"You want to go to lunch, venerable trappa Dazi-Kawa?"

"Yes-you-pay." He always said that when he thought something might cost money. Some people called him "Holy Monk Yesyoupay," and he would say that his real name was Charlie now. "Me Charlie who plays monk Dazi-Kawa sometimes, but *really really* Charlie." If asked what *really really* meant, he would say "means nothing" and laugh and dance. He liked dancing with my wife, not an ordinary party dance but a stylized series of contained movements of joy. He moved in with us whenever he came down with flu and had my wife cure him with chicken soup while he taught her how to embroider holy images on linen. He would play Tibetan sacred music on LP records that he had me order through a special music store. He particularly liked music played on clarinetlike instruments cut from human thighbones. "Cut them out of body," Dazi said. "Before vultures eat corpse. Tibet always recycles."

We usually had lunch at the same Chinese restaurant, and one day Dazi told me he had made contact with all Tibetans in Holland and wanted to invite them for a Sunday zendo service to be followed by lunch. "Only fourteen. Two *lama*s, ordained priests, one high lama, translating texts at Leyden University. They come in robes, yes? Some women, they nurses now. Young women. You like."

I suggested that he should go for the women. I was married.

He smiled his appreciation. "They already spoken for by other monks. Me late."

The zendo service, with the *rimpoche*, a "living Buddha," a recognized incarnation, presiding, was an event that impressed us Dutch "nihilist Buddhists." The high lama wore a gold-embroidered vest over his purple-and-yellow robes. The monks chanted in bass voices; I couldn't figure out how they did it. Dazi-Kawa's speaking voice was fairly high but here, between the smoldering incense and flickering candles, he was booming like the thirty-foot-long mountain horns I had seen in documentaries filmed in Tibet. The rimpoche also had a bass chanting voice. During meditation he sat up straight (most of the monks and lamas slumped somewhat) and emanated light and energy. When he slid down from his cushions at the end of a two-hour meditation, he was old and feeble again, but he wouldn't let me drive him to the little restaurant that I had reserved for the occasion. The Tibetan nurses, also in robes, supported him as he moved slowly ahead, leading the procession through the alleys of the inner city. I walked right behind him, giving the nurses directions. As it was

Sunday morning not too many people were about, but a uniformed constable who recognized me as a fellow member of the Amsterdam's reserve police asked if I needed help bodyguarding what he recognized as an Asian religious party. I told him we were going to have a Cantonese lunch and that the old man with the full white beard was a living Buddha. The reserve constable, a biologist during his regular working hours with interest in the unusual, came to attention, saluted, then bowed, before marching ahead to show official welcome to the distinguished foreign guest and his entourage.

The zendo, kept impeccably clean by us under Dazi's direction, the altar the trappa had so admirably arranged, the silence and stillness observed by my fellow Dutch students while meditating, the police escort, the quality of the Chinese food, and the perfect service performed by the Buddhist restaurant owner and his family, seemed to impress the rimpoche, who gave me an introduction to a Tibetan temple in England, initiated and run by another recognized incarnation. "This might be helpful to your direction," the old man said, smiling. I thought I might try a Zennish answer. "I sometimes think there is no direction, sir."

His noble face assumed a serious expression. "Which no-direction do your refer to? In my school of thought we classify nine hundred and ninety-nine different ways of no-direction. If you attach importance to them I can mail you a paper." His sudden smile seemed to indicate he wasn't too attached himself. I felt encouraged. My experience so far with Dazi and his lama and trappa friends seemed to show that Tibetans, although light-hearted and friendly, are set in their methods when it comes to walking the path. Things were to be just so, and they had holy books to prove that. Dazi often spent hours in the zendo by himself, reverently lifting oblong loose pages of his ancient Buddha book, muttering the texts, telling me he was memorizing thousands of stipulations of his religion's approach. I interrupted him once, pointed at his papers, and said, "All yak-shit, venerable superior brother Dazi-Kawa." He didn't catch my meaning but I had brought a pair of cow horns, now held them above my head, squatted and made farting noises. Dazi was interested. "Really? Buddhist rules are cow dung? Who says so?"

"Maybe not dung, but Buddha himself said written rules are superfluous," I said. I told him about the Chinese "Monkey" book where the monk and his assisting ape, when they finally reach Buddha Land, are given all the holy texts of Buddhism in three wicker hampers.

Dazi had heard about that. "The *tripitaka*."

Three baskets of Buddhist doctrine, to take back to China. On the way down from the Himalayas a storm grabs the baskets and the papers are blown about. The monk, wailing as usual, gets Monkey to help him gather as many as possible and put them back in the baskets. Monkey says, "Sir? Have you noticed these papers are all blank?" Back they go to Buddha Land, to get the teaching in print, but the Buddha, instead of apologizing for giving them nothing in the first place, tells the monk, "the blank paper contains my true teaching; rules that can be written down are superfluous." The monk loads his doctrines on his white horse, bows, and leaves. Monkey leaves too, but looks over his shoulder and smiles at the Buddha. The Buddha smiles back. He holds up his hand, with three fingers stretched up and the index and thumb touching.

I demonstrated.

"Okay," Dazi-Kawa translated. He had seen the hand-symbol, or *mudra*, in town, after a soccer match, when the Amsterdam team had won.

"You agree?" I asked.

"Maybe," Dazi said seriously. The rimpoche also looked serious when I brought up the matter of no-direction, of being there already, of the Heart Sutra, saying, "And there is no path." But what did I know? I didn't want to match my lack of insight with the supreme enlightenment of a rimpoche, a recognized incarnation, a living Buddha, translating the subtlest of texts from Sanskrit and Tibetan into English and, eventually, probably, into my own guttural Dutch. I thanked him for his introduction to his colleague in England. I planned to go there. I wasn't hung up on Zen. I only wanted insights. Maybe the goal does sanctify the means, any means, like burning statues made out of butter, dancing lama dances with my wife, and being massacred by the Chinese.

Rimpoche smiled sadly. "Massacring Chinese are Buddhist lesson."

It's the Only Way Rimpoche Could Stay Here

This was the sixties. England still had trains pulled by coal-burning locomotives, and waiters in railway uniforms came around pouring hot tea, sugar and milk already mixed in, from dented kettles into chipped mugs. The Tibetan temple was in Scotland, in a converted mansion originally owned by a single and childless nobleman, a former sahib, feeling sorry for having exploited the Far East, who had willed it to the Buddhist cause. The train chugged between low green hills stuck mostly in dense fog. Dazi-Kawa had been hoping for snow, but it was still autumn. There were Scottish long-haired cows with wide faces and impressive long horns grazing wet fields. "Yaks!" my trappa companion shouted as he jumped up and down in his seat. He opened the window and mooed at the cattle. They looked up languidly at the wildly waving figure shouting at them in Tibetan. "Everything all right?" a passing conductor asked. "Yaks!" Dazi-Kawa whispered. "It's all right," I said, "He's homesick, you know."

The conductor didn't know. He stayed with us until Dazi calmed down.

Dazi-Kawa, trained along strict lines in the rigid Potala, was upset by what he called "sloppy routine" at the young Living Buddha's temple, and left, after a few days, to be with the British superstar he had met in Amsterdam and would soon be serving in her villa outside London. Before leaving the Scottish/Tibetan retreat he told me I had come to the wrong place. Dazi had bristled whenever he was with Rimpoche but I liked the abbot, a well-built, majestically robed presence in his late twenties, with a bittersweet orange complexion and "angel" eyes that reminded me of the singing cowboy Roy Rogers' musical gaze. Women loved the mere sight of Rimpoche. Men were also attracted by his powerful aura. He had briefly welcomed us in the hall, saying he would have more time later. Dazi was talking to his countrymen in robes while a very short Englishman, also in robes, showed me my room. The British monk spoke with an Oxford accent and underlined most of his statements with sweeping gestures. Henry (he had a Tibetan name too but he always looked more like Henry to me) didn't have the full use of his legs. I had hardly unpacked my bag when he was back, supporting himself on one crutch and pointing at me with the other. "Rimpoche will see you now." He made his message sound very special. I thought he was right. It's not an everyday event to meet with a high priest from this planet's most remote country. I said so. Henry smiled gravely. "And a Buddha to boot."

Rimpoche received me in a large room lavishly furnished with oriental rugs and gilded altars. There were framed photographs of oriental sages in robes on all walls, and a life-sized black wooden Buddha sat on a structure of polished marble. I prostrated myself as I had done in Japan when I had to greet high-ranking priests and thanked him for allowing me to stay at his temple. There were no seats, so I knelt. "You're comfortable?" Rimpoche asked. I told him that I was used to being uncomfortable by now, after zazen practice. He asked me questions about Zen training in Japan. I soon realized that he knew more about koans than I would ever know and that he only seemed curious in order to lure me out. What was I doing at his temple? I said I was trying to "walk the way." He smiled. "How interesting." Rimpoche spoke impeccable English, learned, I heard later from the English monk, at a choice British university in a remarkably short time. He had also obtained degrees in art, philosophy, and religion. As a recognized incarnation of a fully enlightened spirit, he had apparently equipped himself with a brilliant mind. The English monk dropped his crutches, knelt, and served tea from a porcelain pot. He left the room swinging his little body backward. "Henry wants to go to India to be holy," Rimpoche said when the monk was still within earshot. Rimpoche had a boyish grin and a pleasant voice. "Do you have a particular personal problem? You are looking for a solution? You want me to help out?"

I thought of the "father of surrealism," Marcel Duchamp, photographs of whose work I kept on the walls of my study at home. "There is no solution, for there is no problem," Daddy of Dada said when asked whether he experienced difficulties when creating works of art titled *To Be Looked at (from the Other Side of the Glass) with One Eye, Close to, for Almost an Hour* and *Why Not Sneeze Rose Selavy*. I didn't quote Duchamp, although I thought, and still think, that his answer was correct, that there really never was a problem and that the so-called solution is only required when looking at things through the distortion of ego. Things are just fine, only our selfishness makes them wrong. I usually fully believe that, until I see a dog on a short chain or a baby seal wailing for his lost mother. Seal pups can be saved these days—there is a place in Massachusetts that picks them up and takes care of them—but dogs on short chains are legal in my home state and their owners can be violent and short-tempered. Horrors like that start me rethinking my position. "There is no problem?" I ask my distorted ego. "Tell it to the dog, sweating on a hot porch, short on water."

I told the recognized incarnation, squatting behind his red lacquered table, that I had no personal problem worth discussing. I would just like to know for sure. "Know what?" "That there is no purpose." "You believe there is no purpose?" "I would like to know for sure there is no purpose." "Why would you like that?" "Because, if there were a purpose, it would all be too unacceptable."

"Unacceptable like what?"

"Well," I said, "like the Chinese genocide of your people."

He shook his head. "Tibet is finished." His eyes were sad, but the smile was the same as the smile on the black Buddha's face behind him, expressing, it seemed to me, not acceptance but beyond-acceptance.

We had more tea, poured by Rimpoche himself this time, and he told me about a movie he had just seen on the life of T. E. Lawrence ("I like action") as a British hero during World War I. Monk Henry announced dinner, and we all went to the kitchen for an extended meal, a buffet of rice and side dishes ladled into wooden, clay, and plastic bowls. The chopsticks looked home-made, whittled out of wood scraps. All the meals were served this way. Everybody, guests included, in turns, helped Rimpoche and his monks cook, serve, and clean up. Whenever a meal was ready, whoever had cooked it hit a gong and people would troop in. We could sit where we liked and leave when ready. I remembered my Zen meals in the Kyoto monks' sodo: no talking, head monk starts first, each movement, each utensil, each bowl is regulated.

Monks in black robes eating mechanically from black bowls. Bells and clappers rule beginnings and ends. No women. No kids. The monastic dog gets yelled at until it leaves the hall, snarling protests. Laymen dress in black jeans and sweaters. The jikki-jitsu, Zen officer in charge of the meditation hall, gets up, everybody gets up, he marches his men to the zendo, marking time by hitting a hand bell. Cling-clang. Sit. Back to your koan. Never mind blood-sucking bugs. Hold on to your bowels; you can release tension during the next toilet break. The flies will be waiting.

Wandering about the Tibetan grounds after dinner, I met a thirty-year-old Swedish woman with several teeth missing. She was feeding her donkey and told me the animal had pulled her all through northern India in a cart. During the journey she had given birth to two sons; she couldn't remember who were the fathers. "What did you do for money?" I asked. She said her father sent her traveler's checks to the next stop, which she would mention in a postcard. She only needed small amounts—he didn't mind, her father was loaded. Her boys, two toddlers, intelligent and healthy-looking, brought a bucket of cool clean water, some crackling fresh hay, and tasty-looking feed in a bag. The donkey nuzzled their eager faces. He had a nice face himself. I scratched him between the long, short-haired ears.

Ingrid asked what I was doing at the hermitage. She didn't wait for an answer. "Not waiting for Godot, I hope? Godot never left. You know that, don't you?" I laughed politely. "No, really," Ingrid said, "he is you; you are he." She held my wrist. "I am he, too." I liberated my limb, mumbled something impolite in Dutch, and continued my search of the terrain. Unsolicited instruction never fails to annoy the nonenlightened. Screwing around on a donkey cart south of the Himalayas, would that be the answer? Maybe as good as any. The Dutch customary mode (early to bed early to rise, work and save, if you pay attention the queen will give you a ribbon) had never done much for me.

Wasn't I interested in ignoring all values? I wondered what my father would have thought of Ingrid's alternate lifestyle. He might not have disapproved, not at the end of his life, anyway. I didn't see him die but my brother told me that Dad had asked the ceiling, "But what else could I have done?" He had been a hardworking businessman all through his adult life, an occupation that kept him tense and unhappy. My mother told me that my father never wanted to be happy, just "useful." Which he was. How so? Well, he helped essential goods to be distributed all over the world, useful ingredients that make life better, like, for instance, pepper. She said my father was instrumental in seeing that everybody got a fair share of pepper. I was a small child and had tried pepper on a boiled egg, imitating an older sibling, and had licked it and hurt my tongue. When I tried to blow the rest of the pepper off, it made me sneeze into my food. Some years later, being driven to school, sitting next to the driver, I heard my father and a colleague reciting figures in the back of the car. I asked the driver what the figures referred to. "Prices and available tonnage of pepper in various parts of the world," the driver whispered. He told me that the firm my father directed was trying to corner the pepper market. Cornering the market means buying up all available product, holding on to it for a while, then selling it off at inflated prices. I realized my father was a member of a selfish conspiracy manipulating a commodity man can live without but has gotten addicted to. My mother called such an activity "useful"?

Once again I had been seriously misled. I told the driver that I was considering disowning my no longer useful father. He said to delay that temptation, for I was still a helpless teenager and my father was paying for food, housing, clothes, medical treatment, and schooling. "How will you make a living without at least some education?" I thought I didn't need to learn languages and mathematics to become either a tramp or a cowboy. "Tramps see the world and cowboys get to chase Indians that fall off their horses."

"Illiterate tramps sleep in the rain, cough, and spit up blood," the driver told me. "Nonmathematical cowboys get dust up their ass while driving cattle through deserts." He advised me to become a corporate driver. "You hear stock-market tips, convert your pitiful savings into fortune-making options. Sell into strength. Retire early. Sit in the sun in France."

He was my hero, until, five years later, while hiking, I saw him at his home in a Mediterranean resort, swinging listlessly in a hammock above a pile of Heineken empties. He burped when I asked him what was up. "Not much," his companion said. "He just lies there."

What to do with my life? Was I better off paying donations to Tibetan guides on the spiritual path to show me what was really going on, so that I could finally experience truth on an essential level? Could Rimpoche deliver on the pricey enlightenment program as described in his leaflets? For the time being I enjoyed myself. Early morning services at the temple were impressive. Fragrant incense smoldered on at least six altars and the monks chanted as exotically as my Zen tutors in Japan. Apart from the English monk Henry, Ingrid and her sons, and three elderly Englishmen with military mustaches, I didn't see any westerners around. At breakfast Henry told me that there were some ten British and American acolytes in retreat, doing Rimpoche-prescribed spiritual exercises in small cabins built in the woods behind the main temple. He told me the temple specialized in solitary retreats under Rimpoche's guidance. First retreats were just a few days, but in the small dark buildings farther back in the woods, the exercises might last months, even years. Future monks were given meditation subjects and programs specifying what they were to do hour by hour. Get up before daybreak, quick wash, two hours of meditation, breakfast, gymnastics on the balcony, more meditation, lunch, and so forth. Naps were included, and there was also some night rest, but overall the menu was definitely

Spartan. "Tough," Henry said. His own ordeal, a three-month sojourn, had nearly driven him crazy. "Does anything happen?" I asked. Henry had experienced ecstasies. "Afterward just about anything gets easy. If you can do that kind of stuff you don't worry much about other trouble."

I remembered Han-san in Japan saying, after a particularly arduous three-month training episode, that he had died. "I'm dead. I am beyond ego now. I'm no longer here. I'm free. Nothing can happen." He lay on the floor of my room, being a corpse. Then he jumped up and clowned around. "Dead men gather no karma."

I walked into the Scottish/Tibetan woods. At the third cabin, an unpainted rectangular shack half hidden by a towering oak tree, I saw a frantically waving hand. I went over to the open window and a young man looked at me worriedly. "Where is my breakfast?" I told him I was just a guest. The acolyte, wearing a robe, told me he used to be called Tom but would soon, after his present ordeal, be given a Tibetan name, Jetsun. "They're giving me a hard time. They keep forgetting to feed me and I didn't see Rimpoche today, who is supposed to come by daily." Tom checked his watch. "Should have been here hours ago. Is he drinking again?"

I had missed Rimpoche at the morning meditation in the main temple room. Maybe he was ill? Tom didn't think so. "Partying," Tom told me. "He does a lot of that. He has friends in the village. Girlfriends, too. Here and there. Can you get me some breakfast?"

I went over to the kitchen and arranged poached eggs, toast, marmalade, two types of cheese, fresh orange juice, a tulip in a tumbler. I brought the tray over to the recluse's shack. Later during my stay I attended a ceremony where Tom became Jetsun. I made several trips to the retreat afterward, combining spiritual welfare with a small-scale business venture in England. Jetsun was learning Tibetan and studied scripture. He showed me passages wood-block-printed in beautiful flowing script. We sometimes meditated together, trying to ignore the crows that made a racket outside. He told me about the carousing going on in Rimpoche's quarters, saying he was often in on it himself. "Part of the discipline here. We overcome our hang-ups." He joked. "I just get hungover. Pot helps me contemplate but I don't know about alcohol, all that Scotch whiskey messes things up and when he is drunk Rimpoche grabs all the girls." I didn't pay much attention to Jetsun's complaints. I didn't look for what Jetsun called "our shadows." I liked the painted woodwork in the large temple room, the potluck dinners with everybody smoking self-rolled cigarettes afterward, the sutra chanting and the relaxed group meditation without patrolling back-whacking clerics. Whenever Rimpoche talked to me, my spine became alive with an electric current. Ingrid and her sons had taken the donkey cart home to Malmö, but other unusual characters kept coming and going. The place was like a spiritual version of the British sitcom *Fawlty Towers*. Being out of my usual business routine in itself was a pleasure.

Rimpoche never singled me out, but monk Henry came over to my room one evening, announcing solemnly that the Living Buddha was ready to accept me as a lay disciple welcome to come over for sojourns whenever my family and business duties could be temporarily lifted. I refused because I had just gotten a letter from Sensei. Sensei, during my sojourn in Japan, was a disciple of Roshi, my Japanese teacher. We had been in touch. Roshi had died by then and Sensei, in his letter, told me he had left Japan after completing his long training and set himself up as a Zen master in the States. He was willing to teach me. It seemed logical that I should see him there and perhaps consider moving to America altogether and becoming his disciple. I told myself I would be following a karma line that had passed through Roshi.

Rimpoche accepted my excuse and said he would like to

meet this Sensei, as he was looking for a contact in America. "Maybe we exchange students." It all seemed to fit very nicely. He took me out for a drive in the country. Living Buddha and Dutch merchant riding in a Rover.

Rimpoche had been given the car by his support group of London-based backers and often took girl disciples on outings to the seashore. A month later, when I was in Amsterdam, an accident interfered with the temple's routines. Rimpoche, driving home after visiting a pub in a nearby town, accompanied by his favorite mistress, hit a tree. "Alcohol-related," Jetsun wrote. "That elegant Rover got wrecked. Beth is unscathed but Rimpoche hurt his spine and has lost the use of his lower body. The doctors see little chance for improvement but he says he'll be just fine, that he'll cure the spine by curative concentration and shamanic treatments. He rides about in a wheelchair; Beth takes care of him. Meanwhile things continue. Soon most of us will lock ourselves in for retreats. Trust you are sitting too. Keep up the good work."

What good work? I was creating and distributing expensive articles for doing needlework, products in vogue with ladies of leisure. In my second routine I patrolled the inner city as an auxiliary policeman, showing the way to lost tourists, mostly to the whore quarter, for that was where everybody always wanted to go. I conducted Sunday morning sessions at our quaint zendo. I was a husband and a father. I sent Jetsun a picture postcard of a gabled house with women in the windows: "*You* keep up the good work—here we are just keeping busy."

Rimpoche showed up in Amsterdam. He had discarded the robes of the order he had headed (saying he considered himself a nonranking civilian now). His Brooks Brothers suit made him look like a golden Miles Davis. Mistress Beth, in a miniskirt, pushed the august presence in his wheelchair. The spectacular pair caused a stir at Schiphol Airport. Rimpoche wanted to see the

District that very evening. He wanted my car parked at the edge of the quarter, preferring to view the luscious scene from his wheelchair. He looked around curiously, taking sips from a bottle of tax-fee cognac, bought on the KLM plane, that fitted a metal holder attached to the wheelchair. We also drank glasses of foaming draft beer in pubs. It was spring; decorative fruit trees were in bloom in the old city. Black thrushes sang from gutters and rooftops. "You're doing good work," Beth said to me. "This sort of outing makes him relax. He needs that for his concentration. He is willing his legs to function again. He is actually getting better quite quickly." They stayed in a hotel, and my wife and I drove them around for a week. Rimpoche drank constantly and became irritable at times. My wife was about to whap a fly that was bothering her during dinner and Beth screamed "Don't kill a sentient being!" and got whacked over the head by Rimpoche, who told her to keep her voice down.

The pleasure quarter was a magnet. Soon after Rimpoche's visit I was walking Sensei through alleys where young, almost nude women contorted their bodies behind glass. He asked if there were also attractive young men in windows. I said there were. "Show me," Sensei said.

I could see myself facing the Hereafter Judge. "What did you do on Earth?"

"I guided Buddhas."

"Where did you guide these Buddhas?"

"Along the canal quays of Amsterdam, Your Honor."

"Looking at whores?"

"Looking at whores, sir."

"Did they physically possess these sentient beings?"

"Right," I said. "Sentient. Aware. Buddhas took a vow when they were still bodhisattvas. They were supposed to save all aware beings before becoming Buddhas. But they didn't save them, Your Honor, they did—"

"Did they physically possess these sentient beings?"

"I don't know, Your Honor. Not when I was with them."

"What do you think?"

"I think they probably went back later on their own."

"And you think that was your task on earth—guiding Buddhas to carnal pleasure?"

My Calvinistic core came to life, but my wife soothed my concern with what enlightened spirits should and should not enjoy in the way of carnal pleasure. "Buddha had a harem when he was a prince."

"What do *we* know?" she asked. "And what do we *care*?"

Dazi-Kawa did care. He wanted nothing to do with Rimpoche's carnal aspects. He didn't care for Sensei, either, and refused to sit with him in our alley zendo. Dazi left to join his British superstar again. He sent me a postcard showing London Tower. The text said, "I am happy now." I heard that he only wore his robes during ceremonies in the star's private shrine, and wouldn't discuss religion with anybody but his mistress. "They have a deal," my informant said. "She takes care of his needs here, he gets her an easy passage to some really nice heaven."

Half a year later, Tom/Jetsun, now a monk but dressed in designer jeans, a dress shirt, and a linen jacket, showed up to have his turn being guided through Amsterdam's maze of twisting alleys. As we walked and stared, Jetsun kept offering me cookies he said he had baked at the Scottish temple. I began to feel giddy quickly. I had smoked hashish in Africa (and had not particularly liked the experience, preferring dry Cape wine, both heady and legal) but didn't know the drug could be eaten. "You should have told me," I told Jetsun. "It's a crime to dope a person without his consent. We could have been drinking cold Dutch gin." My legs had become elastic and weren't too willing to make it to the nearby zendo. We floated above our meditation cushions while Jetsun's fourth-dimensional voice told me about his recent trip to

India, as Rimpoche's assistant. They had meditated in Himalayan caves close to the Tibetan border and everything went well there: Jetsun experienced insights, shape shifts, realizations, liberations, journeys into the realms of supreme understanding, but later, staying at houses of supportive Buddhists in Calcutta, Rimpoche was drinking heavily again and caused problems by bothering female members of the households. After being evicted, once again, by an angry father and husband, Jetsun confronted his out-of-control mentor. Rimpoche got upset. "He told me to get away from him," Jetsun's booming voice (my drugged ears acted up strangely) told me. "He tore up my plane ticket. I was begging in the streets for a third-class passage on a rustbucket cargo." Jetsun made slow movements with arms that looked impossibly long to me. "A white beggar in Buddhist robes in India's poorest city? And Rimpoche still seducing wives, daughters, servant girls, nuns, the *cat*?" Jetsun's thundering laughter shook the zendo. "He is impossibly attractive!"

I wanted to say "And we are here, stoned—should we follow a fool?" My lips were numb. While I struggled, trying to communicate, I could hear other voices talking. Nietzsche was saying, "There are no absolute values, only temporary values, which indicate no more than a self-appointed status." David Hume: "There is nothing there, never was anything either—we made it all up." The humanist lady on Dutch TV: "But we can always behave nicely, can't we? Please?" Baba in Logan Airport: "Don't bring me your disappointments and personal doubts. None of that stuff should be of interest to you, either."

Rimpoche's eighteenth high-lama body (he had been recognized seventeen times before), weakened by hard living, died when it was barely in its forties. I mentioned the fact to a Mohawk shaman who was lecturing in New England and was staying at our house. Her eyes widened as she took in the pictures I was drawing for her. Abandonment of faithful disciples. Fornication.

Mismanagement of funds. Drunken levity. Lethal addictions. A radiant irresistible presence, whose teachings now illuminate the globe. A flawed personality? Riddled with bad habits? Is a saint subject to rules?

I knew she had studied in Mongolia, with both shamans and Buddhist lamas. Rimpoche, a native of eastern Tibet, came from both a Buddhist and a shamanic tradition.

There was a silence. I knew the Mohawk lady as a caring woman, a mother, a wife, responsible about financial matters, a productive gardener, politically engaged in the welfare of her race, also a dedicated teacher and guide to any serious student who sought her out. The shaman composed herself. Her large black eyes sparkled. "Yes," she said, "I've heard of that happening before. It probably was the only way Rimpoche could have stayed here."

THE MASTER'S FEET TURN RIGHT
IN FRONT OF YOUR HEAD

Bobbie-san, the American monk who had finished his Zen training in Japan but fell out of grace because he refused to pursue a
career as a teacher, showed up again at our house in Sorry, Maine.
There had been a lapse in time that didn't seem all that long but
did encompass more than twenty years. Our bodies didn't fold in
and out of vehicles easily, we couldn't read without glasses, we
both sported goatees that looked like they had been sloppily
whitewashed. I used a cane when going uphill. "How are you
doing?" I asked when he got out of his rental car. He said fine,
but he looked frail to me. He told me he was reliving his past
and wanted to stay a few days. He moved into the outbuilding
he had used before and spread his sleeping bag on the not-too-

comfortable bed. There was still the same propane cooking gear and the little woodstove, both somewhat rusted. We ate mushroom sauce over noodles, slurping noisily, and remembered the bad old days, when we were more arrogant, had more energy to be ego-driven. He narrowed his strange green eyes, incongruous in a face that had become almost completely oriental after adapting to forty years of Japanese settings. He grinned after we had ceremoniously burped and were sipping tea. "Are you going to test me again?" I said I wouldn't dare.

During that first encounter I had "checked him out" in various ways, thinking I shouldn't miss the chance to figure out a saint, sage, or whatever term applies to a human in the selfless state. Sensei had done extensive Zen training too, but as a layman, and had never received a seal of final approval. Bobbie-san had successfully completed first monkish, then priestly, sodo and zendo training. To me, in those earlier days, that would equate with having learned all, ergo, there you are. No more koans. So then what happens? (I knew better by now—nothing much happens, except some people go crazy, like a lady disciple of Sensei's who, released after solving all koans in Sensei's book, found freedom too much to cope with and needed serious treatment for the rest of her life.) During that first meeting I was sure I couldn't compare my spiritual insights with Bobbie's, but I had thought of another way to analyze his status. I had always been led to believe that "realized" Zen men are superbly practical. The egoless being cannot be beaten. No matter what comes up, they spread their spiritual arms and sail gracefully across the hurdle.

Zen-Rambo.

I called Bobbie-san that now and he laughed, "I boasted, didn't I? Zen-Rambos don't do that. You found me lacking."

The lacking was mutual. What kind of a host uses a guest for a spiritual guinea pig, but that's what happened. During that first encounter I used my own habitat to test the allegedly enlightened visitor. Living in the country, I exercised by cutting, splitting, and stacking quantities of firewood for our stoves, sole providers of heat during long winters. It was early spring then, still quite cold at night. Before Bobbie arrived I made a fire in the little stove that heated the guest cabin and left him kindling and matches in a closet. Dry firewood was stacked outside, in a little shed partly hidden behind bushes. There were some old newspapers too, left in a drawer of the desk. I didn't tell him where to find any of these items. Next morning I found my guest miserable and cold; the fire had burned out and he hadn't thought of locating either burning materials or matches. "Did you look?" The cabin had kerosene lamps that he couldn't light for lack of matches, and he couldn't find the matches for lack of a flashlight. A Zen monk traveling into rough country without a flashlight? Really, and I had left him a flashlight, in a fairly conspicuous place, but he still didn't see it.

Failure of first test.

I had left baked beans and other staples in the cabin that he couldn't prepare because he didn't know how to get the propane stove going. Not just because he couldn't find the matches, but because of the intricacy of manipulating the stove's two faucets. Another miss. Well, never mind. Maybe he had been too tired to bother. Time for breakfast. I took him to town for a late stack of blueberry pancakes. He was very shy with the waitress, a pleasant enough woman who inquired about his Zen robe. I had to speak for him. It was obvious he had a problem with buxom, happy ladies. Now, could be chop wood?

Yes. Bobbie-san told me he was an expert. He was the chief wood chopper at the Nagasaki sodo, expert with the long-handled ax. He was good with mauls and wedges and sledgehammers too, of course. He was rubbing his hands. He was going to show me.

As soon as we reached my work area, he went for my collection of twisted logs and gnarled roots that I had been avoiding.

I told him to leave them alone; he would break his back on them. Once the stack was big enough I planned to rent a motorized splitter. "Besides it will take a month if you do that by hand." He brushed my warnings aside. "I can do it. Please let me." Sure. Behold the bodhisattva dealing with an oak log with grains twisting three different ways. He hammers in a steel wedge carefully, tapping it with the rear side of a maul. Then he aims to hit it with a mighty swing of the sledgehammer, but he misses, and breaks the brand-new tool's handle.

He also broke the maul's handle. Then he broke the ax. Then he lost both wedges, in the snow somewhere.

He had excuses. He was wearing new spectacles he wasn't used to, so his sight was blurred. He would pay for the damage. Nah, that wasn't necessary. But he had money, he assured me. Nah, it was okay. Laymen are supposed to support monks. I went to town to have my tools repaired after watching him starting up my tractor, to which we had hooked a cart. He was going to take wood I had chopped before to the house and stack it there. He told me he knew all about tractors, for he had been the tractor driver at Nagasaki sodo for several years. The tractors there were Japanese high-tech. My American machine was quite simple.

There was a fire engine in my driveway when I came back from running errands. Bobbie-san had driven the tractor through a heap of dry wood chips, some of which had gotten stuck in the exhaust area of the tractor. A small fire had started up and instead of using the extinguisher that hung in a conspicuous place in the nearby garage, he had run to the house to call my wife to help out. By the time she got herself out of the house, the flames had found the tractor's gas tank.

Bobbie-san offered to pay again, but I had good insurance.

That evening, to get rid of my angry and his shameful feelings, we agreed on discussing Buddhist subtleties in the gazebo on the shore of the bay. We took the little propane stove down to heat water and I made tea laced with half a jug of jenever, the strong gin of my native land. Bobbie-san said we were going to be Musashi. Musashi is the great Japanese medieval hero who overcame his ego to turn into the best sword fighter in all of the land. The exemplary warrior killed every opponent who dared to challenge him, after trying to warn the poor chaps off, but they foolishly kept coming, to be felled with one clean swoop. Musashi's brilliant sword practice is often compared to Zen meditation. In keeping with a scene in the book, I had brought strips of cedar bark to burn in a hibachi so that we could warm our hands in between drinking the hot jenever. Burning cedar bark, according to the Musashi book, produces delicate flames and a perception-enhancing fragrance. The spirits seemed helpful, for the night was clear with a rising full moon. There was no wind and we could hear the slow lapping of waves, almost reaching the moss garden below the gazebo. The setting was ideal. We couldn't miss; I was sure I would substantially benefit from this auspicious meeting of qualified sage and advanced student. Bobbie-san and I bowed to each other, filled each other's glasses from the jug warmed on the stove, bowed again, raised our drinks, swallowed, coughed, smiled wisely. As we kept consuming more alcohol to keep our exchange properly elevated, I hardly noticed that we were staggering about making exaggerated gestures to underline unclear suggestions and shaky propositions. We kept repeating ourselves. We kept agreeing. We laughed a lot, then we became maudlin. I had intended to use the Mu koan as the exchange's focus but neither Joshu, nor the monk, nor the dog would stay in their places. Finally I dropped and broke my glass, stumbled and hurt my leg on the splinters. Bobbie-san slipped too, and burned his backside when he sat down in the hibachi. Our improvised bandages didn't hold. We lost our way in the woods on the way back to the house.

"Did the Mu-puppy bite you?" my wife asked after she helped me into the house and took care of the wound.

No more tests were staged for this second visit. I didn't want to ask, but Bobbie-san told me that his quest for women, when he returned to Japan after his first visit to my place, hadn't worked out either. He did try. He temporarily changed his robes for regular clothes and didn't shave his skull for a few months. He was a professor of oriental studies getting to know the lay of the land. Staying mostly in inns while traveling all over the country, he had an easy introduction to many available women, who were pleasantly surprised by the interesting foreigner's fluent Japanese. There were lots of flirtations, any kind of opportunity—all leading to nothing doing. "I'm not gay, either," Bobbie-san said. "I'm sure I would like nothing better than to to get to know women intimately."

"Did you give up?"

He sighed. On getting laid? Possibly. On solving his philosophical problem of "the great doubt"? No, but he no longer knew how to go about it. He was a kind of a loose priest now, sometimes wearing his robes, sometimes not. He had gotten various degrees and served as an assistant professor of religion at colleges. He had inherited money, so there was no need to go all out for a living.

"Do you sit?"

He told me he wished I hadn't asked him that. It was too personal a question. Did *I* sit, now that I had definitely left the obligatory training? See? I didn't want to give a straight answer either. He had sat for maybe four hours' average a day for twenty years—that's nearly thirty thousand hours. Not even the Buddha had sat that much. For fuck's sake, man . . .

Okay, okay. I was sorry I asked.

"Up in a tree," Bobbie-san said. "Up in a tree."

I knew the koan. It deals with answering a question. Master Kyogen said.

> "You have climbed a high tree. You slip. You clench a branch in your mouth; your arms and legs have no support. Now then, if I stand under the tree and ask you the meaning of Buddhism . . . eh? If you don't answer you evade my question. If you do, you drop dead. So how will you answer my question?"

Was Bobbie-san testing my insights now? I gave him the right answer. Flailing my arms and shaking my leg, I pretended to have a big object in my mouth and to be talking around it. "Ungggghunnggghu."

"Remember the rest of the koan?"

I did—one doesn't forget these twisted stories easily, not after having carried them around for months until the teacher gets bored and provides the answer himself:

> An older monk says to Master Kyogen, "Never mind up in the tree, please, Master, let's hear about the time when your fellow is not up in the tree." Kyogen laughs. "Ha-haha!"

"And how would you explain all that nonsense?" Bobbie-san asked.

"Please," I said. "Do I have to pass the koan again?"

"Not in Zen-speak." He seemed excited. "In plain talk. Tell me. Up in the tree, under the tree, what were those guys talking about?"

I was amazed. This was against all rules. For two and a half millennia Zen folks have been refusing to use plain talk. What were we supposed to be now? Renegades? Were we betraying the cause? Wouldn't Manjusri's sword flash and cut out our hearts? Wouldn't the bodhisattva of compassion, the seductive Kwan Yin, spit hot tar on us? But what did I care? I had never been good at keeping secrets. Up in a tree, like many others, is simply a trick question. A man hanging by his teeth from a high branch will fall anyway. He is about to meet with deep trouble. His mumbling isn't an expression of the meaning of Buddhism, but a request for help. The master should bring a ladder.

The second part of the koan shows what happens after the man gives up his hopeless position. Now that he is down, he is either dead or in pain. A good answer would be to pretend to be dead, or to say "Ouch, that hurts."

Bobbie-san said never mind whether he was still sitting in meditation. Maybe he was, maybe he was not. There was no pain there. What did hurt him was to have to live without getting laid, ever. Up in a tree he was asking for the pleasure of being with a woman. Down under the tree he was complaining about his eternal virginity.

I was trying to think of "the other side of the coin" (there's always another side to the coin). Should I tell him about the suffering caused by being either a carouser or a dutiful householder? I was still thinking when my guest told me about his teacher's jubilee. Bobbie-san had been literally pushed out of the monastic gate for refusing to be his master's spiritual heir, but time heals even Zen-inflicted wounds and after ten years there had been a reconciliation. The old abbot was about to celebrate forty years as a teacher. His heirs and students, including Bobbie-san, came to the mother temple. The buildings had been cleaned and redecorated. Choirs chanted sutras. Dancing priests performed elaborate rituals. Incense smoldered everywhere. The current class of monks had pulled every last weed from the moss gardens. Giant golden carp swam between the water lilies in cleaned ponds. Windows and doors were repapered. Paths were raked. All the lay supporters of the temple came with their families, most of the women in colorful clothes to suit the occasion. There were lots of little kids. Dignitaries, both clerics and government officials, delivered congratulatory speeches. The cooks had prepared the vegetarian foods that are the fame of Zen kitchens. There was plenty of sake. Most priests were aware that the master had a drinking problem, which had been getting worse over the years, but because of all the revelry no one was paying attention. Suddenly, the master's quavering voice, amplified by a powerful sound system donated by one of the great electronic corporations, reached every corner of all the Zen buildings, gardens, and yards. "I want to get m-a-a-a-a-a-r-rrried," the master was chanting. After that he sobbed loudly.

"No!" I tried to cover my ears and eyes simultaneously.

Yes. The old drunk felt lonely, Bobbie-san told me. Zen masters can marry, but those who choose to become monastic teachers usually do not. The sex drive, Bobbie assured me, does not get sublimated spiritually, as religious textbooks claim. Sexual longing is programmed into human genes; frustrate it and it becomes demonic. Twisted devils bide their chance to get out in the open. The master's demons kicked down the door of their cell at the great jubilee party. There was the party-pig sage; clutching his microphone, keeping up his wailing and sobbing while his monks rushed about trying to switch off the loudspeakers.

No! I was still covering my eyes. This was as bad as the Zen archer I had seen on Dutch TV, a Japanese archery-adept in robes, bowing, kneeling, dancing, praying before he pulled his bow's string and had his arrow miss the target completely. Colleagues in the Amsterdam constabulary saw that show. "Wasn't that what you studied in Japan? Zen? Is that why you are bad at pistol practice?"

Bobbie-san's low voice kept extending the plot line of the

Nagasaki jubilee party. The master was taken to his quarters and kept there, supervised by strong monks, until he sobered up. A committee of high priests faced him a few days later. "No more drinking." The master slipped a few times and was institutionalized for a while. Declared sane and sound, he returned. Monastic training started up again. The monks, after early morning meditation in the zendo, lined up in the corridor leading to the sanzen room, kneeling on the hardwood floor as they had so many times. The head monk is first in line. It is 4 A.M. sharp. There is a bell, hanging inside a heavy wooden stand, at the head of the line, and as soon as the master rattles his little hand bell in the sanzen room, the head monk hits the big brass bell hung in its heavy wooden stand and goes to face the master. Only this time there was no tinkling of the master's bell; there was only a long, lengthening silence.

Now what? Another exercise in humility and patience? That's it, the master is devising a so far untried situation to break through his disciples' egos. Let them wait for a change. Show them they can depend on nothing, not even on monastic punctuality. Their knees burn on the hardwood floor; the first mosquitoes of the warming summer day are biting the monks' faces, hands, and bare feet. A very long hour passes. The cook monk and his assistants, kneeling behind the head monk, should be done with sanzen by now and at work in the kitchen, boiling gruel and water for the tea on slow stoves fueled by twigs and leaves. Still no sound from the sanzen room. Finally the cook monk leaves his position and shuffles humbly to the head monk at the head of the line. He whispers. "Head monk–san, excuse my speaking out of place, but I feel something is wrong. Please check what has happened to our teacher."

The head monk still hesitates. How can he strike his bell without being prompted by the master's hand bell? The cook monk prods the head monk with a hard finger. The head monk reluctantly gets up and walks to the sanzen room. He enters and prostrates himself three times, he kneels on the mat. The cushions on the platform ahead are empty, but there right in front of his face, the bare feet of the master turn slowly in the room's draft. The head monk bends his head back. Above him, dressed only in a *fudoshi*, the little white penis-wrap used by old-fashioned Japanese men, the master's small body is strung from a rafter.

All activities have their shadow sides, but it seemed to me that Bobbie-san, during his long stint at Zen discipline, had been singled out for excessive horrors. His apparently successful career gave him rank and respect but no answers to his questions, if I was to believe his dark mutterings. His report sounded like a tale of not only physical but spiritual impotence, of obedience to worthless causes, of being steered into instead of out of his self by a bogus teacher. "More bullshit from the bogus captain" was his favorite George Carlin quote, taken from a tape he put into my TV set. We watched the comedian tell us that airline "captain" titles are bogus because the pilots were never commissioned. He then tells us about an episode where an airline pilot instructs passengers to put their heads in their laps so he can crash the plane safely. "How apt," Bobbie snarled as he switched off the tape. "I never noticed the Buddha commissioning my teacher either."

In spite of the gloomy aura that enveloped Bobbie's being, I was glad to see him again. "Otherwise you are okay?" I asked. He laughed sadly. "Not really. My body is giving me problems too. You want the long list or the short list?"

We went through his collection of physical complaints. Much can be learned from listening to other people's tales of woe. "It's like watching a movie," I had been told by Rimpoche during a lecture in Scotland. "You watch and laugh and cry and applaud and boo, but it doesn't really touch you because it's some other illusive ego identifying with some other nonsense." Bobbie laughed when I shared that wisdom. "As long as it isn't you, right? What's so wise about that?" "Rimpoche was getting to that," I said. "The idea is to see my own life the same way."

Bobbie and I talked about what we are not. We are not our minds. We are not our bodies. How both are inconsequential parts of our beings. Here for sixty-seven years or so, gone after another ten years or so. Just like movies, long movies. Nothing to do with us, the real us, the pure being. But just a minute now, wait for the next severe depression, off to the shrink. Wait for the next allergic condition that doesn't respond to over-the-counter medication, a strained ankle, a mysterious chest pain. Off to the emergency room we go.

"But it's still part of the dream," Bobbie said. "No. Seriously. The visit to the doctor is part of the dream too."

Dreams. That was the message his dead master had left for anyone who had ever been involved with him through his long lifetime. The teacher's body, after having been cut down from the sanzen room's ceiling, was cremated, and Bobbie attended the memorial ceremony in the temple's dharma hall. The head monk, wearing his full set of robes, showed the congregation a large roll of paper. He unrolled it while monks chanted the Heart Sutra behind him. The scroll, in the calligraphy of the dead master, showed a single character, *yume*, "dreams." "This is," the head monk told the supporters of the temple, "all our master saw when he looked back on his life. He saw dreams without permanent importance. Maybe they seem to matter while we are dreaming them, but soon they'll waft away and break up in the process. Mental dust to mental dust. You will notice that he did not even sign his summing-up of yet another human life that will soon be forgotten. He showed us his final enlightenment that way, for most high priests, their tails of ego stuck solidly in mud, like to sign their creations, to try to leave something of their interesting personalities with us. There's the artful flourish of their expert brushes and the flaming red of the seals of their office to remind us that they were on earth too once. Our master didn't do that. See how simple his calligraphy is? No frills? He truly had no ego."

"More bullshit from the bogus master?"

Bobbie thought that the deceased had done his best. Maybe the best wasn't good enough. But he had cut his ego down some.

"Sure," I said to Bobbie. "Minimal ego, but when you refused to be his successor, an ahead-of-time projection of future Buddha Maitreya, he didn't take that so well. Out you went, meboy. Never to return to Daddy's lap."

Bobbie kept defending the master, whom he had intimate contact with, on and off—on, mostly—for a very long time. A kindly old man really, who should have married and had some home life to relax in after a strenuous day at sanzen. And besides, Bobbie said triumphantly, nobody really has an ego. Samsara is an illusion, has no true substance. It was quite in keeping with the master's job to leave us that "dreams" character to help us see the illusion of our lives, the way he had seen his.

I was still grumbling. As an Amsterdam policeman I had seen

dead bodies hanging from nooses and considered the dreadful scene an unkind good-bye to the unfortunates who found them. The third time I didn't vomit, but I woke up screaming for several nights afterward. The monks must have been freaked out when they saw their living example unexpectedly changed into a disgusting object.

"Over and done with," Bobbie-san said. "He is gone. We're still here. 'Step step step, the early morning breeze'—didn't Hakuin say that? Meaning: Let's get going, see what we can do with our opportunities today? What was that about you saying you would take me out boating between the magic islands here? Is today a good time?"

It was. He was right. He was on holiday from his various jobs in Japan, and as a good host I should share local pleasures with my guest. It was one of these rare days on the Maine coast that the sea lies flat under a pure blue sky. My boat was ready at the dock. A push on the starter button and the old diesel courageously roared to life. Yo ho ho and a Thermos flask of green tea. I had told Bobbie I had given up alcohol since his last visit. "You ever drive this big wooden tub drunk?" Bobbie wanted to know, watching the powerful wake behind us as we left the cove, sipping the tea I had poured. I said jenever and boating don't mix in Maine. The ocean around these parts is unforgiving. Razor-sharp shoals lurk, hardly visible under a few inches of water. A fourteen-foot difference between high and low tides causes fierce currents, which often form maelstroms. Pay no attention for five minutes after having checked position and charts, lured to feel sure that there will be a hundred feet of sea under the keel for miles around your vessel, and suddenly there is a telltale white fringe where waves break over rocks or the wreck of another vessel whose skipper once felt safe. The area is known for sudden rain-and windstorms. "But not today," Bobbie said.

Definitely not today. It was a beautiful day at the height of the season. We listened to a pleasing voice booming out of the weather radio on the bridge. "Enjoy yourselves, tourists and locals," the weatherman was saying. "It doesn't get any better on our beautiful coast. Your chance for living life the way it is supposed to be. Sail or hike to your heart's content. A sumptuous day. You could even try a little cool swimming. Clear skies all around. No strong winds expected."

We motored and drifted in turns for hours, Bobbie-san and I. We caught mackerel and broiled them over a wood fire on the beach of a little island, to go with pickles and fresh bread we had brought in a hamper. We studied a pair of nesting eagles through binoculars and, eventually, with the naked eye, for the big birds seemed to welcome our coming close. A little later Bobbie shook my shoulder and pointed with both hands. A pair of pilot whales, quiet giants of the oceans, swam next to the boat, one port side, one starboard. Hundreds of eider ducks sat on the slow swell of the ocean, the males contrasting their white and amber feathers with the luminous dark blue of the ever-supporting sea. Floating loons showed off their bright red summer spots. "This is it," Bobbie sighed. "We've finally got it made. Ignore ever failing humanity. Just swim between the advanced water beings." We did that, too. A big bull seal came close, breathing importantly through his heavy mustache, but I told him it was okay, I wasn't after his wives, no matter how invitingly they rolled their glistening bodies around me. He dived under me for a moment and his sleek skin rubbed against my feet.

We thought we might find a pleasant place to drop the anchor and spend part of the night philosophizing under a full moon. While we cruised around slowly, enjoying the setting sun, a loud roll of thunder made me look back. A pitch-black cloud rose without warning behind the pale green ridges of the shore. It came straight at us. In just a few minutes the sea frothed all around the boat, which no longer felt safe in spite of its wide beam and powerful engine. "Toy of the waves," Bobbie-san shouted. Visibility was under a hundred feet except when lightning flashed, showing ominous shapes in the sea ahead. Waves or rocks? I was on the fly bridge above the cabin, trying to check a chart when a "cat's paw," a bundle of whipped-up air, grabbed the paper and took it off into the darkness. I still had radar, but the screen was below in the cabin. I tried to switch the steering from the bridge to below, but the mechanism got stuck and this was no time to fuss with screwdrivers and pliers. I had no choice but to have Bobbie, an inexperienced sailor, steer the ship from above, while I watched the radar screen below, trying to coordinate green blobs with what I could remember of the chart. Where could we be, exactly? Was that pear-shaped blob Pond Island? If so, we were heading for some sunken ledge, which we could avoid by veering sharply to port, but only if the other blob was Tinker Island, and Tinker has several sharp rocks on its north side that we would be heading for at speed. We couldn't go slow because of currents and the windstorm combining to push us sideways against ever growing waves, which would make the boat list uncomfortably, even might capsize her altogether. Bobbie could only hear me if I shouted in his ear, so I had to run up and down the steep metal ladder connecting the rear deck with the bridge. House-high waves, by then, were breaking over the boat. Both Bobbie and I couldn't see without spectacles, and our glasses were being splashed by salt water. I found a plastic can with fresh water to wash off the salt. Bobbie and I kept passing the jug, until a wave grabbed it and swept it overboard. We had to use spittle and our handkerchiefs instead.

I wasn't sure I had enough fuel to keep us going on that raging sea. With the throttle wide open the engine would be sucking the tank empty within the next two hours or so. The old diesel was still thumping below our feet, but I knew how tender it had become after a lifetime of service. There were several parts that needed replacing but I hadn't worried too much, planning to take the old tub out during daylight and fair weather only. I normally didn't race the engine, and the thinning exhaust tubes should be holding for another season. My radio worked; I could always call the Coast Guard. I had flares, an inflatable raft, enough canned beans to last for a week, a flashlight. I could refill the jug from the pond on Pond Island. There had been all those safeguards and none of them were of any value now. No Coast Guard helicopter would ever see us in this harsh weather, and if we used the raft it would puncture itself on the shoals. A drowning man doesn't eat canned beans. My flashlight wouldn't float for long before getting smashed on a ledge. The flares, fired from their little plastic pistol, would soon sizzle in the driving rain. "This is bad," I shouted in Bobbie's ear. "Think of something helpful," Bobbie shouted in my ear. I told him I was too scared to think of a thing that could save us from doom. "Not one single thought?" Bobbie shouted. I saw the reference. This was indeed a time to quote koans. "Mount Sumeru!" we shouted together.

Once a monk asked Master Ummon, "When not one thought rises, is there any error?" Ummon said. "Mount Sumeru!"

Going beyond thinking made us steer a safe course. Soon I began to recognize patterns on the radar screen. At least we were moving into the right direction. The storm was pushing the boat to the dock behind my house, still some eight miles away and through an area that had little water at the present low tide. The next challenge would be to find the channel. "Next barrier," I shouted. There were still sharp shoals ahead, invisible even on radar. Maybe I could remember their locations. The channel wasn't altogether safe either, for it was narrow and silted up to less than five feet in parts, and the boat drew four and a half. We had a following sea with fifteen-foot waves; if we got stranded on the bay's gravel bottom the waves would smash the boat's old boards. Seawater in Maine is cold even in August. The human body doesn't withstand low temperatures too well. I had heard of several cases of saved sailors slipping away even when taken care of in the hospital's emergency unit. "What's the third barrier?" Bobbie-san shouted. Zen obstacles always have three stages. I didn't answer—I was too busy looking for channel markers on my screen. They didn't show. The screen was never too clear at the best of times, and the markers could show only as small dots. There were lots of dots, caused by spray perhaps, or floating objects, or by drops of salt water on my glasses. I joined Bobbie and shone the flashlight from the bridge. The markers have strips of plastic that reflect light. Going as slow as we could, hoping we were aimed at the channel, the flashlight might show us cans and nuns. After what seemed to be a long time the first can showed. I remembered compass courses that would lead to following markers. I watched the compass while shouting instructions at the steering Bobbie-san. "Just a hair to port now, okay, little bit to starboard now." We did run aground once, but I pushed the throttle while a huge wave lifted us. The boat bumped along until she found another few inches of water to float on. After the last red nun, bobbing crazily on raging mud-colored waves, the depth finder showed ten feet. "Second barrier taken," I yelled into Bobbie's ear. A tear in the clouds gave the moon a chance to show my dock.

Bobbie was asking about the third barrier again. I didn't think there was one. We were home; all we had to do was tie up, switch off the engine, walk up the path, find our beds. He insisted that we couldn't be safe yet.

Bobbie was standing at the bow, ready to jump on the dock to tie the painter to a cleat when demons started howling. The fierce shrieks made him lose his balance. He fell off and I had to shift into reverse so as not to crush him between dock and boat. The tide was coming in by then and the current spun the boat around, and I had to switch the engine off so as not to behead him with the propeller. He shouted and I threw him the cork ring that hung from a hook on the bridge. Its line wrapped around my leg and almost pulled me in too. The flashlight showed me the source of the hellish commotion: half a dozen large raccoons standing on rocks next to my dock, gesturing and yelling in eerie high voices. It could be that the looming, thumping boat distracted them from a ceremony, or a party, something very important in the life of raccoons, for they were certainly angry. Bobbie was swimming to the shore, but the raccoons wouldn't budge, even when I shone the flashlight into their eyes. He had to return to the boat and grab my hand so I could pull him over the railing. We had to concentrate on sending friendly thoughts to make the raccoons scamper off into the alder bushes.

Then, suddenly, everything was just fine. The clouds evaporated, the moon shone quietly, the boat nudged herself gently against the dock and allowed herself to be tied down for the night. There was no damage. The bilge pump was squirting water out of the boat's side, burbling musically. The winds died down. "You had a nice sail?" my wife asked sleepily as I slid between the sheets. "There was hardly any wind, was there? And you had the moon. I saw some lightning far away and I was going to worry but then I went to the dock earlier on and everything was so calm." She caressed my arm. "I love nights like this—they empty the mind. No thoughts rise."

"No error?" I asked.

"Mount Sumeru," she said. She had been a Zen student too, but I had never heard her say "Mount Sumeru" before. "But the peak never shows for long." She kissed me. "Sweet dreams."

THREE NICE THINGS

There is a Dutch saying: Small kids and bad drunks speak the truth. Maybe former Zen students, their minds somewhat cleared from pretense, tend to report accurately too.

At a Zen center in the Four Corner area that I visited after seeing it mentioned in a chamber of commerce pamphlet—*Zen Insights, Views & Art*—a secretary nun introduced me to the abbot, an imposing figure dressed in a sky-blue robe. When I complimented him on his beautiful temple, he whispered "Ah" and pointed at something behind me. I turned around, didn't see anything that hadn't been there before, and looked back again. The master was no longer there. The nun said he was a magical figure. Did I know he could outsit anybody in the temple's zendo, seemingly asleep but fully focused on the Buddhist void? When not meditating or disappearing, the master liked being silent. Wasn't silence, she asked, always the best answer? "To what?" I asked. She put a finger across her lips.

The place was jumping. I counted some forty uniformed monks and nuns bustling about. There was a bakery open to the public and the store displayed Zen sayings hand-written in bold letters, by the abbot, on scrolls—*Man of no rank, the fresh morning breeze, enter fire not burn enter water not drown*—and wooden hand-painted statues of meditating monks with MADE IN INDONESIA labels. The moss and rock gardens imitated famous Kyoto examples. The architecture of the buildings was oriental and there were stone pagodas, Buddha and Kwannon images, and wash-basins displayed on areas of gravel raked in geometrical patterns. A wooden ego-slaying demon whose club foot trampled a human-shaped self grinned from his pedestal. The nun said the demon was hollow; if a visitor stuffed a banknote into his mouth the donation would be used for a holy purpose.

During a second visit there was a FOR SALE sign on the drive-way, crossed over by a strip of paper that said SOLD. The park was overgrown with weeds, the temple's once perfectly papered doors and windows tattered. A large raven sat on the main gate. It croaked when it saw me. "How do you like my pal?" the gatekeeper asked. "Nevermore has been around since the fore-closure." The keeper said he was a former monk, hired as a care-taker until the new owners claimed their property. "It'll be a facility for the mentally impaired."

I told him I had been a Zen student once. Only his T-shirt, he told me, was still Zen—it came from the former temple store and showed an unshaven face peeking from a hollow tree. "When I joined the brotherhood I was called after this master. He took his name from Mount Daizui, where he lived in the hollow trunk of a tree. Daizui figures in a koan. You want to know?"

I said I wanted to know.

He told me what the koan was.

"When the big bang reverses and the cosmos leaves us, will we go too?" a monk asked Daizui.

I had to come up with a comment. "Say something," the former Daizui who now called himself Jim told me. I got annoyed. "Sure."

"Sure what?" Jim asked.

I said, "Sure we will go too. You don't want to stay, do you?"

"Stay where?"

I shrugged. "When the whole thing goes, we go too. Nothing is permanent." I was sure Jim was kidding. There is never any place to stay in Zen. Not even in hollow trees, like his austere example, Daizui, who apparently liked staying without comforts.

"You knew the koan, didn't you?" He seemed impressed. "That's what Daizui answered. Same as you said just now. 'We will go too.' How did you know that?" I said it's smart to get angry at any Zen-produced question that wants the student to hold on to something. Anger cuts through the cleverness of the mind. Up pops the correct answer. It won't help much, because real insights are never koan-produced, but it gets the student to the next koan.

Jim and I were soon into denouncing our former teachers. Jim raged about the master's habit of answering questions by being silent. We came up with a suitable koan:

A monk inquired, "What is the meaning of Daruma going out to preach Buddhism to the Chinese?" The abbot was silent. Another monk asked another teacher, "What was the meaning of the abbot being silent?" "Maybe he didn't know," the other teacher said.

I asked Jim what had happened to the silent master of the now closed temple.

Jim took my arm and walked me to the edge of the cliff the temple was built on. "He's setting himself up again. I saw his ad in a holy magazine." He cupped his hands around his mouth. "Folks? Step right up. Silent Treatment saves your spiritual ass at a discount-count-count-count." He dropped his voice. "He'll be raking it in again and spending it faster. Another Mercedes, more first-class returns to Paris, a gold Buddha statue, piles of other stuff nobody needs out of the holy catalogs." Jim shook his fist. "Master Dipshit-shit-shit-shit?" He took another deep breath. "May the force be against you-you-you-you." Jim had aimed his voice at the ravine below us. The echoes were clear.

The performance made Jim hungry. There was a Mexican takeout nearby, operated by an older woman whose brusque manner reminded me of the tea lady penetrated by Master Joshu. Carrying lunch, Jim took me back to the mesa that the former hermitage was built on. Hiking on for a mile or so, we reached a promontory overlooking a plain of flowering saguaro cactus and various kinds of spiny bushes. Jim was still complaining. "Dipshit deserves all the pain I can send him." He turned to look at me. "I gave my power to the place here. My time, my energy, anything I had. He abused my trust. He's like the psychiatrist who doesn't break his patients' identity transfers. If I don't stop him with my curse, he will make zombies out of new disciples."

It was time to unwrap the enchiladas and twist the caps off the ginseng soda. Nevermore had followed us and sat on a blackened beam, part of a former cave dwelling. The raven seemed friendly. Jim called its name and it flew over to inspect the food, pecking daintily at his share before he grabbed it.

Jim said the cave had been used by a shaman, according to the lady below at the takeout. He thought that the shaman's power had shown itself as a bird.

"A raven?"

She hadn't been specific. "She doesn't say much," Jim said. "I buy all my meals there. She sometimes doesn't even bother to make change. I think she mostly speaks Spanish." He pointed at vultures planing on air currents. "Doesn't she look like them? They call them *zopilotes* here."

The raven muttered. I offered more food, but it wasn't interested. It kept croaking at us. "Nevermore," Jim said. "Sure. I know. We're done here. She sent you with us so we could say good-bye."

Jim was telling me tales of Master Dipshit and his own wasted past and I told him tales about Sensei and my own wasted past so we could blame self-chosen teachers. The raven flew away. We needed a change of air. "Nothing good ever happened at your temple?"

Jim said no. I insisted. The atmosphere was getting too unpleasant. He gave in. "Two good things happened. One that helped me get to the center, the other broke the routine for a bit."

The first good thing was the way Jim got to Buddha. He had loaded up credit cards and wanted to clear them before being a monk on a mountain. Work at a building-supplies store generated only minimal wages. He proposed to his new idol, "Help me pay my debt and I'll try to be empty." The next day a customer, an antiques dealer, asked Jim out for a beer. The dealer told Jim a nearby church was about to be decommissioned to make room for a food franchise. The church contained a large stain-glass window showing Christ on the cross, a valuable piece dating back to Mexican times. He couldn't take the glass down alone. He offered money, the exact amount Jim owed Visa. A sure sign.

"Theft?"

He hadn't asked. The dealer and Jim wore uniforms, name tags, professional-looking belts with the right tools in holsters.

They used a pickup truck marked STAINED GLASS REPAIR. Everything worked out like clockwork. "The destination was halfway across the country. We had a nice long scenic drive afterward, stayed in inns, ate in good restaurants."

"The second good thing?"

Was even better, Jim said. There was a nun at the center who, to please the teacher, had taken a vow of silence. One day a phone call came in saying that the nun's father was dying at some considerable distance. The teacher told Jim to drive her there in the temple van.

I saw what was coming. "You two had sex."

"Can you imagine?" Jim said, "We were both in robes. Nothing was said because of her vow, but the tension built up for hundreds of miles before anything happened. First she went oral. We made it to a motel and the next morning she talked. She said the release of tension had made her see through Dipshit's manipulations. She bought regular clothes at the nearest thrift shop. She made it in time to see her father die. She inherited his house. She is still there. She went back to school—she's going to be a teacher."

"Zen?"

"Elementary school," Jim said. "She is also getting married."

Those were nice things but there were only two, and the atmosphere was still heavy as demons of discontent moved furtively around us. The raven had come back. We needed a third nice thing and I thought of a ceremony I had heard Jetsun talk about at the Scottish Tibetan center. In order to get rid of anger, a quiet place is to be found and a cleaning ritual is to be imagined. Jim, Nevermore, and I sat in the cave and called on vultures and others to surround us. We took off our clothes and burned them, together with our hair, on a fire built of twigs between us. Next we peeled off our skin and gave it to the birds. Our muscle tissue and arteries followed, being picked up by snapping beaks. The vultures fed on our hearts and other organs. They ate the bones we tore out of our skeletons and cracked and broke into bite-sized pieces. Finally our hand bones walked themselves over and were eaten too. It took about an hour to get rid of ourselves.

"You hardly moved," Jim said. "I thought you said you were bad at sitting."

He hadn't moved much himself. I had been aware of Nevermore hopping around us, but he wasn't there when the vizualization was over.

We walked down from the mesa and bought Polar Bear ice cream at the Mexican takeout. "We enjoyed our cleaning-out at your shaman's cave," I told the old woman. She looked away. "*La limpia, señora Zopilote,*" Jim said. "Cleaning up with your namesakes."

Maybe she smiled. It was hard to see with all those wrinkles. "*Váyase.*" She told us to go, to eat our ice cream outside; she was locking up for the day.

EMPTINESS IS FORM

Hindu, Taoist and even some Buddhist scriptures (Buddha, reputedly, never answered questions about the afterlife) mention after-death bardos, "low spheres," purgatories—which the recently dead have to traverse—and "high spheres," heavens that prepare the soul for rebirth. Only arahats, bodhisattvas, saints, sages, ("remarkable men" as the Armenian sage Gurdjieff would have called them) are excused from going through the purgatories. All others spend some time in these forbidding halls, tunnels, and caves, where they face guardians, judges, gods of wrath. The gods often take animal forms and seem frightening. Experiences in these spheres may seem unpleasant to the passing soul but are no more than reviews of scenes from its recent life on Earth. The guardians carry mirrors that show what really happened, display true motivations, analyze past activity, expose false insights, unravel chains of effects caused by the soul's previous deeds and attitudes. The criticism involved may appear to come from the judges, but is really the soul passing judgment on itself. The ego will cringe, but is advised by the guardians to pay attention humbly and accept even the harshest verdicts, so that, cleansed, it can pass on to the next "house of hell," until, eventually, it is released to the highest, least-lowest, purgatory, where dancing skeletons serve up a feast. From there the soul is free to reach the higher, "heaven," spheres.

Some souls don't do well in the lower bardos. In spite of all mirrored evidence, ignorance may persist, defense can be stubborn, and the soul may even attack the deity that seems to be giving it a hard time but is, in fact, no more than its own reflection.

This, I understood from the literature, would be the exception rather than the rule. Inappropriate behavior in hell, however, happens. If it does, the soul blocks its entry to the next sphere up, and, after an unhappy interlude, reincarnates directly into another physical life that comes loaded with bad luck.

Normally, however, the soul does succeed in being purged and manages to "regain its original golden color." In its clean form, it now enters the higher bardos. Again there are many separate levels, ranging from the pleasurable to the instructive. In a lower heaven the soul may (there is no obligation) enjoy any pleasure it either remembers or imagines, no matter how sensuous or "forbidden" by its own former standards. Higher heavens replace regular pleasures by the subtleties of abstraction. Gradually there is deepening of appreciation for philosophy and the arts and sciences. Eventually the soul is ready for spiritual instruction and readies itself to accept an auspicious rebirth. Things are getting better and better.

I didn't think I had to worry about the heavens, apart from the fact that they would be temporary and might be hard to leave. The hells seemed of more immediate concern. I wondered if there would be a special hell dedicated to adjusting wrong insights into the void, the great emptiness that I had been trying to visualize, fantasize, actually reach, for as long as I had been thinking. Had I fallen for taking the easiest of all ways out? Did my soon-to-be-passed-on soul excuse immorality by an absence of morals?

In a manuscript on Native American insights (*Dreaming the Council Ways* by Ohky Simine Forest) I saw a Maya reference that, at first sight, looked discouraging. The reference is to one of the lower bardos (the fifth). The sphere is called Cave of Nothingness, also known as the House of Darkness. The deities that are in control of this dank hole are owls, big birds of silence. In this region there is a confrontation with the inner belief, picked up mistakenly during an egocentric life, that "nothing matters," that "there is no life after death." The soul survives the ordeal by "keeping its inner light alive." If, at this stage of the review of its earthly life, the soul remains in denial, it cannot make the next move (which has to do with facing its ancestors) and will, after having a bad time with the fearful owls, be reborn to relive the ordeal "in the flesh." I read that, like at any stage of the path, all is by no means lost here, provided the soul persists in keeping up its search. The four great owls that face him, in spite of their seemingly gloomy presence, mean well. Also, like all gods met within the lower spheres, they carry a mirror to reflect the soul's state of development. If the soul observes the "spiraling void in the mirror," the image will help him meditate on his last life's unhappy misconceptions.

Perhaps here, in the House of Nothingness, lies a particular risk Zen students face: the possibility of being absorbed by the shadow side of negation, a weakness I saw in several teachers and also in my own approach, preferring self-centered lazy indifference to a state of mental freedom.

The Heart Sutra that keeps Zen hermitages going with its punctuated early morning chant of "There is no suffering, no cause of suffering, no cessation of suffering, and no path" starts off with describing how the bodhisattva Avalokitesvara, "cruising in the perfection of understanding," realizes that "form is precisely emptiness and emptiness precisely form."

Roshi Robert Aiken of Hawaii seems to have taken the latter part of this statement as a motto for his battle flag: "Emptiness precisely is form." Once we have meditated on the ultimate reality of the void, the zero of everything that confronts us, and are liberated of the weight of having to carry a universe on our shoulders, we can turn around and see that emptiness projects "nothing" into a myriad of forms. How to deal best with these forms? Zen teacher Aiken does not accept the status quo of strife on earth and does his utmost to help his students and readers to gain insights that will help them to improve any form-shapes they deal with on a daily basis. So do all teachers, including the seemingly negative guides, assembled on these pages from bits and pieces of authoritative apparitions I happened to run into. Master Dipshit, Sensei, Bobbie-san's suicidal abbot, monks, nuns and laymen, and even some aspects of the Tibetan masters I describe here are collages, put together to carry certain ideas. The actors on this stage aren't linked too closely to my actual life. That said, there is an exception. Feeling the need for at least one ideal, lovingly humorous, detached and courageous teacher, I was happy to draw on some of my experiences in Japan with a person whom I still consider to be a superior man. Roshi told me "all lessons are fun," including the debilitating Parkinson's disease that was making such a mess of his bodily functions. I think "Rimpoche" would agree, although I'm sure that the Living Buddhas I had the honor to meet with were beyond all lessons. "Sensei," the way I built him up, or down, might Zen-theoretically agree that lessons are fun, but his habit of walking about in a black cloud belies that supposition. Baba, with his "just be" doctrine, certainly believed that all situations should be dealt with diligently and as perfectly as possible, whether it was clearing tables at JFK Airport or instructing the unenlightened at Logan Airport.

I wonder now whether my original idea of having Zen prove that "nothing matters" in order to avoid all pain and suffering in any situation was all that smart. Aiming for the void, for "being cool," for making nightmares disappear by pricking their merely existential bubbles, the Mu koan seemed to be the ideal tool. It was also an ideal trap. Understanding on a low, merely intellectual level, of the total lack of substance, whatever substance, to anything at all, can lead to callous behavior by doing nothing. Shortly before Allen Ginsberg died, I heard him chant in Central Park to the tune of his little pump-organ. The key line that stayed with me was "It is never too late to do nothing." I thought then, Yes, I am too busy, step back, let it go, never see anyone again, be a hermit, go shopping once a week at 6 A.M. when the market opens, talk to seals and loons and dolphins only, and when the body gets a little more decrepit, take it out in a rowboat aimed at the horizon and blow it up with dynamite. Carrying that plan, I wandered to the other side of the park and heard jazzy music. There were festivities celebrating some special occasion, and thousands of uniformed schoolkids marched up Fifth Avenue in neat formations. There were adult bands too, horsemen, dressed-up folks on National Guard vehicles. There was a lot of energy about, but some participants were clearly exhausted. A dozen obese girls shuffled along, weary of dragging their weights, and ahead of them there were some little guys, ten-year-olds maybe, carrying drums. They were tired too; they had probably been at it for hours, walking down from Harlem, doing "hurry up and wait," assembling in a dusty dry place, having their teacher fuss over them, and now there were all those other smart schools and they were just that little group, special husky kids and their undersized musicians—might as well quit now while they were still on their feet. As despondency was about to strike I saw the chief drummer suddenly change his mind. Why do nothing? Why not pull down all the energy of the universe? Some huge ray of power hit that diminutive player of a snare drum, a flash of divine lightning, and immediately his sticks hit the wooden sides of his drum, smartly, a touch of staccato—*tick tack*, get the show going here—using a harsh dry rattle, and then all heaven burst loose as his mates got going around him. There was an instantaneous fusing with the spirits of Philly Joe Jones, Art Blakey, Max Roach, and other angels that got into their awakening souls, and the small band was doing solos and joint rhythms harmonized with tricky compositions on a trumpet another boy found under his jacket that spat out the hoarsely cutting notes of Miles Davis's "So What." The plump girls behind him were dancing their divinity in perfect step, trembling the brilliant cadence within their bodies, emitting rays of light that swept the Fifth Avenue audience for miles.

Emptiness took form.

The way out of the big hole of darkness guarded by the Maya owls that urge, by holding up their mirrors, the passing soul to replace his indifference by detachment, and to lose his ego to perform better the tasks set by his karma.

Were the koans I studied so painfully only designed to enter the big hole? The master urges, the head monk scolds, and the jikki-jitsu, Lord of Discipline, does his macabre police dance to push the student off balance while whacking him with the keisaku, Manjusri's sword. The subject of all this violent attention hangs by his teeth from a high branch, totters on a cliff watched by a hungry tiger (another tiger slavers below), has to stop the Tokyo-bound bullet train coming at him at full speed, is told to carry the weight of the loss of all he had, is stripped of his rank in front of the troops, is yanked by the ego-tail so that his peers can laugh when he falls over backward, observes his body being fed to vultures, is made a fool of by a nasty old lady, never gets a straight answer to a simple question, doesn't get served his dinner on time, and is transferred, even fired, when he shows signs of comfort. The teachers he tries to emulate turn into cardboard silhouettes or irrational martinets. Their corpses hang in front of his face. Again new gurus appear. Refuse to zombie up to the current master and get shunned for your troubles. May as well get numb, give up, join the audience at Fifth Avenue, eat Polar Bear ice cream sold by the tea lady who locks you out of all insights while looking away, but never mind, and the light strikes and the little boy plays the drum and his big sister Kate shimmies right behind him determined to keep it up through all hells and heavens, right out there, on a Buddha cloud with a smile, and for no particular reason, either.

Fall into the big hole of not caring, fly out on the cloud of detachment.

The cracked mirror, the empty mirror, the mirror showing true motivations, no mirror at all, no handle no frame, free passage to now, to here.

THE *Koans*

Gozo's water buffalo bull, passing by that window—his huge
head, his big horns, his four feet go by, but that's it, the tail
never shows up. What of that, eh?

"Does the puppy dog have Buddha nature too?" the monk
inquired of the priest Joshu. The priest said "Mu," meaning
"No."

There is a Zen monastery. Tokusan is the abbot, Seppo is the head
monk [abbots teach, head monks are temple managers], and one
day the noon meal is late. Tokusan, holding his bowl, enters the
hall. Seppo says, "I didn't hear the bell announcing lunch and
the gong hasn't been sounded either. Old man with your bowl,
what are you doing?" Tokusan is quiet. He lowers his head and
returns to his room. Seppo now tells another monk, Ganto,
"Tokusan may be great, but he never understood the final verse."

The true practicer of austerities does not fly into nirvana.
The monk who breaks the precepts does not slide into hell.

The priest Sekiso said, "You're on the top of a hundred-foot pole.
Now, how do you advance?"

A traveling monk asks the old woman, "Which way to Mount Sumeru," she says "Straight ahead," he goes straight ahead, and she sneers at his back, saying, "This fine monk goes the same way." The monk, feeling insulted, complains to his teacher Joshu. Joshu says he'll check the old woman out. He visits the tea shop, asks for the way to Sumeru, is told to go straight ahead, the story repeats itself. Joshu returns to his temple and tells his monks, "The old woman has been penetrated by me."

A monk asked Master Ummon (862–949), "What is Buddha?" Ummon answered, "Buddha is a shitstick."

A monk approaches Joshu. "When I bring not a single thing, what do you say?" Joshu said, "Throw it away." The monk said, "But Master, I have nothing. What can I throw away?" "Then carry it along," Joshu said. Hearing the master say the liberating words, the monk became enlightened.

Once you realize your own nature, you are free of "birth and death." When your senses are gone, how do you free yourself?

You beat the grass and probe the Principle Only to see into your nature. Right now, where is your nature?

If you are free from the cycle of life and death, you will know where to go. But when the four elements are separated, where will you go?

When the Dalai Lama smiles, the seals on my shore bark.

"What is the meaning of Buddha going preaching for forty years?" the monk asked Joshu. "The maple tree in the garden," Joshu answered. "Don't use the environment to show people what's what," the monk said. "I'm not doing that," Joshu said. "So tell me," the monk insisted, "what is the meaning of Buddhism, sir?" Joshu pointed at the tree. "The maple tree in the garden."

"You are slandering the old man. I tell you, there were no trees in Joshu's garden."

Master Gozo said, "Even Sakyamuni and Maitreya are his servants. Tell me who I am referring to."

In your physical bodies, right inside your flesh, there is the unrankable being who often goes in and out of the doors of your faces. Who is he? Tell me right now.

"You have climbed a high tree. You slip. You clench a branch in your mouth; your arms and legs have no support. Now then, if I stand under the tree and ask you the meaning of Buddhism . . . eh? If you don't answer you evade my question. If you do, you drop dead. So how will you answer my question?"

An older monk says to Master Kyogen, "Never mind up in the tree, please. Master, let's hear about the time when your fellow is not up in the tree." Kyogen laughs. "Hahaha!"

Once a monk asked master Ummon, "When not one thought rises, is there any error?" Ummon said, "Mount Sumeru!"

"When the big bang reverses and the cosmos leaves us, will we go too?" a monk asked Daizui.

A monk inquired, "What is the meaning of Daruma going out to preach Buddhism to the Chinese?" The abbot was silent. Another monk asked another teacher, "What was the meaning of the abbot being silent?" "Maybe he didn't know," the other teacher said.